# An Organizational Guide to Telecommuting

AMERICAN SOCIETY FOR TRAINING & DEVELOPMENT

# An Organizational Guide to
# Telecommuting

## Setting Up and Running a
### Successful Telecommuter Program

George M. Piskurich

ASTD

Ordering information: Books published by the American Society for Training & Development can be ordered by calling 800.628.2783.

Library of Congress Catalog Card Number: 98-070650
ISBN: 1-56286-086-0

# Table of Contents

# 1

# Telecommuting: What It Is (and Isn't)

*"At first, it's scary."*

—Experienced Telecommuter

## Introduction

Telecommuting. The term conjures up different thoughts for different people. Some anticipate the joy of no longer needing to get in a car to go to work, and others, the tranquillity of not having to live in a cubicle at work. There are those who see telecommuting as a way to be more productive for more hours each day, and others who glimpse it as a chance to work when they're most productive, not when the clock dictates they should. Some believe it will eliminate the need for expensive day care for their children, and others hope it might eliminate the need for a boss. But some workers think telecommuting would be isolating and lonely.

There are bosses who hope it will get workers out of their hair so they can do their own work, and those who hope it will mean they can stop paying rent on expensive office space.

In reality, some aspects of what everyone thinks about telecommuting are true, but some of it is not particularly accurate.

This book describes which hopes are realistic, which have possibilities, and which are unfounded or even in error. Then it explains how to structure a telecommuting intervention for an organization so that the company and the telecommuters achieve maximum benefit. The steps of this intervention include developing proper goals and procedures, methods for introducing telecommuting to the organization, choosing individuals who have the best chance of succeeding as telecommuters, training telecommuters well, training supervisors to help telecommuters succeed, and evaluating the intervention.

The quote at the beginning of this chapter—and those that begin the other chapters as well—is from a description of a telecommuter's personal experience. At first, telecommuting was scary for this particular telecommuter and organization. I hope this book will make it a little less scary for other companies and individuals.

## A Brief History of Telecommuting

Telecommuting has been around for a long time, at least as long as there have been telephones, and probably even longer. The history of telecommuting isn't clear-cut because how one interprets it depends a lot on how one defines the term *telecommuting*. The term has a multitude of definitions. To some people, anyone who works at home is a telecommuter. Following this logic, then, people involved in the cottage industries in the 14th and 15th centuries were telecommuters. This definition is too broad for this book.

Modern telecommuting, as most people define it today, closely mirrors the ascendancy of the computer, and as might be expected, occurred first and foremost in the computer industry. As computer programmers became more and more important and harder to find in the early 1970s, companies like Control Data Corporation (CDC) began to explore the concept of working at home as a recruitment tool. Programmers, who have the somewhat deserved reputation of being corporate mavericks, liked the idea of not being stuffed into a corporate office and being able to concentrate at any hour on their work. CDC's telecommuting policy gave it a competitive advantage for a time in the hiring of programmers.

Shortly thereafter the federal government funded a number of studies dealing with the subject of the telecommunications and transportation trade-off. These studies generated enough interest that some state governments took a closer look at telecommuting, particularly California because of its massive freeway systems, even more massive traffic jams, and mega-massive pollution problems. By the mid-1980s, California had a demonstration project under way that was successful enough for the governor to establish telecommuting as a viable option in disaster preparedness. (Descriptions of these and other studies cited in this chapter appear in some of the books listed in the suggested readings at the end of this book.)

Private industry was also continuing its exploration of telecommuting. Projects at the University of Southern California involving a number of Fortune 100 companies proved the viability of telecommuting in corporations.

The computer industry was soon joined by the telecommunications industry and then by newly categorized information workers in other industries in developing pilot telecommuting projects. Even in businesses where telecommuting was not officially recognized, people were setting up one-to-one telecommuting situations with their managers.

As the 1990s unfolded, issues such as air pollution, population pressures, energy conservation, and other factors prodded industry and government into taking an even closer look at telecommuting as an alternative work process. The 1990 Federal Clean Air Act and the Americans with Disabilities Act have made telecommuting more enticing to businesses from a regulatory viewpoint, whereas simple economics and the need to develop productive, satisfied employees have motivated telecommuting from entirely different levels of the organization.

As the 1990s end and the next century begins, telecommuting has begun to come into its own. Commercials for large telecommunications companies extol the virtues of being a telecommuter, articles in major business publications discuss the feasibility of telecommuting in various business environments, and news broadcasts devote time to discussing how America's workforce is changing, citing numbers like over 11 million "official" telecommuters at work (or not actually "at work") every day.

## Definitions

Earlier I noted that the definition of the history of telecommuting depends on the definition of the process. Statistics on the number of telecommuters, the productivity gains due to telecommuting, even the types of industries involved in telecommuting depend on some preconceived definition of telecommuting.

This book looks at telecommuting basically from a corporate point of view. People who are self-employed, no matter what their business, are not its focus, nor are consultants or others who work for large companies but are not actual employees of those companies. Even official employees of businesses who "unofficially" work at home every now and then will not be discussed.

This book will not consider individuals who are temporarily hired by companies and normally do much of their work at home but have no direct corporate affiliation (in other words, don't receive a W-2). Neither will those modern entrepreneurs who work directly from their homes and are doing everything from arts and crafts to freelance psychiatry be considered. That's not to say that parts of this book, perhaps most of it, will not be relevant to these groups or that they do not make up a significant number of what many experts refer to as telecommuters. It is simply that they are not our focus here.

The focus of this book is (a) employees who work for companies, whether large or small, and sometimes or often officially work at home, and (b) just as important, the companies themselves. As a formal definition for this book, *telecommuting* is a business-centered initiative in which employees who would have normally worked in an office environment of some type are working in their homes for part of the normal work time. This book considers telecommuting from the point of view of a planned organizational intervention and focuses on the telecommuters, their supervisors, and their colleagues who are part of the intervention.

## Nontraditional Work Processes

Because the work associated with telecommuting does not occur in an office environment, it is considered a nontraditional work process. There are many nontraditional work processes. Some organizations use the term *flexible work* to describe an entire class of programs and processes that are nontraditional, that is, that have work aspects outside the "normal" 9 a.m. to 5 p.m. office environment.

From a more theoretical viewpoint, these processes are referred to as decentralized work, under the assumptions that the Industrial Revolution began the centralizing of work (doing away with those cottage industry proto-telecommuters) and that the information revolution is now decentralizing it again (enter the new version of the concept, the telecommuter).

Although telecommuting can exist on its own as an alternative work process, it can also be part of other nontraditional work processes, depending on one's definition of those processes. For example, "hoteling" is a process in which companies rent offices in various geographic areas for short periods of time for employees who do not have actual physical offices because of the nature of their work or because they are on temporary assignment away from their normal geographic region. One aspect of telecommuting is setting up these offices through various technologies so that employees can communicate with the main office without actually going there.

*Flexiplace,* in which people work in one location or another, can include working at home, which is, or could be, telecommuting. If a worker's flexiplace arrangement entails working at the headquarters and branch offices, the person would not be a telecommuter. *Shared space,* in which two or more workers occupy the same office on different days, is an aspect of telecommuting, or possibly telecommuting is an aspect of it.

This may seem confusing, and it frequently is to business writers, statisticians, the government, and just about anyone else who tries to deal with telecommuting and related concepts. One of the first challenges that a company must face when considering telecommuting or any nontraditional work process is to define the concept for its particular business environment. Chapter 3 provides more detail on this aspect of telecommuting.

To allay this confusion, the "Definitions" section was precise about the meaning of telecommuting for the purposes of this book, and it set limits as to what will and will not be considered in this book.

To help keep things straight, following is a list of some of the major nontraditional work processes and some brief definitions that relate to telecommuting:

- Alternative officing
  - Remote work centers are corporate-owned minifacilities away from the main office, usually in the suburbs when the main office is an intercity location. For the purpose of this book, the people who work in these facilities are not telecommuters because they are not working from their home and they are expected to be in the remote work centers or the main office each day, although these facilities are sometimes termed *telework centers.*
  - Shared space is the use of a single office by more than one employee, though not when both are present (or so it is hoped). Telecommuters who usually report to the main facility on a periodic basis can easily share an office. This is one of the real estate advantages of telecommuting, and one of the psychological disadvantages. Scheduling is a major concern with this process.

—Virtual office is an alternative work process in which employees have no actual physical location for an office but "plug in" wherever they happen to be. They may connect from a hotel room, home, a conference room, or even a car. Salespeople often have a virtual office. Because this book focuses on home offices at which employees perform office work on a regular basis, it does not consider virtual offices to be telecommuting functions or salespeople to be telecommuters. This definition may be a bit of hair splitting, but it will make it easier to understand some later concepts. Most of what will be discussed concerning telecommuting is transferable to a salesforce and a virtual office environment.

—Team spacing (group address), a process that has become more prevalent with the ascendancy of teams, provides for no offices for team members but rather a group space that is a combination office and team meeting area. Unlike shared space, team spacing presents no scheduling problems. In fact, it often has no desks or other accoutrements of a normal office. Because telecommuting can include a virtual team process, team spacing can be an aspect of it.

—Hoteling is office space on a temporary basis for employees whose jobs require geographic proximity to a certain area. The space may be in a current corporate facility, or it may be short-term leased space in another facility. It may be reserved for periods of time or utilized on a drop-in basis. Hoteling will not be considered a telecommuting process, but the technology used to create hotel offices at noncorporate locations is basically the same as that used for telecommuting.

—Satellite officing are corporate-owned or long-term leased offices that are not at main corporate locations. They range from single rooms to entire floors. Most often they are for permanent use by specified employees, though they may include aspects of hoteling as well. The key issue for telecommuting is that the employees are expected to be at the satellite office, and not at home. However, a satellite office may be the place that a telecommuter reports to on nontelecommuting days. This concept is often synonymous with remote work centers, though some organizations define each differently.

- Alternative time processes
  —Flextime usually requires an employee to spend a normal number of hours in the office each day, but it allows some choice in what those hours are. Choices might include arriving early, leaving late, or being away sometime in the middle of the normal workday. Flextime is not a telecommuting process because telecommuters by definition spend entire days away from the office. Flextime can be an aspect of telecommuting, however, if telecommuters have the choice of what days they will telecommute or what hours they will be available in their home offices, or both.
  —Compressed workweek is usually a process in which an employee works four 10-hour days or some variation thereof, so that the normal number of work hours is completed in fewer days than the normal workweek. Depending on how telecommuters' pay is calculated and the freedom they are given to choose their own work time, telecommuting can involve aspects of compressed workweeks.
  —Compensatory time is the hours worked but not paid that will be used as time off later. Like compressed workweek, compensatory time is usually not a telecommuting process, but it may be depending on the telecommuters' compensation procedures. It is another one of those policy aspects that a company must decide upon before its employees undertake telecommuting.
  —Core time is a predetermined number of hours in which employees are expected to be at the main work location

when they spend the rest of the normal workweek elsewhere. This is a precursor of telecommuting in which the rest of the time is spent at home, and the core time may be as little as a day or two a month.

- Other nontraditional work processes
  - —Job sharing is a system in which two or more employees share one normal workweek job and the commensurate pay.
  - —Telecommuting is the combination of various aspects of shared space, flextime, and electronic communications to increase worker productivity. I used this definition to reemphasize that telecommuting by itself can be considered a nontraditional work process and to help summarize the concept that telecommuting, as we are defining it, includes aspects of many of the alternative work processes we have just discussed. It can incorporate flextime and core time; it may include shared space, team space, and satellite officing; and it can even encompass job sharing with a disabled telecommuter working at home and a colleague taking care of the office aspects. Finally, the definition is just a reminder that telecommuting is a technological intervention with the overriding goal of increasing corporate productivity.

## Other Terminology

A number of other terms and definitions related to telecommuting are not in the category of nontraditional work processes. Many of these appear in the glossary at the end of the book and may be worth checking before continuing with this book. Following are some of the more important terms:

- computer conferencing
- modem
- videoconferencing
- electronic mail, or e-mail
- electronic bulletin board services (EBBS)

- telecommuting contract
- Americans with Disabilities Act (ADA)
- graphical user interface (GUI)
- groupware
- hardware
- software
- management information system (MIS, or IS) department
- Internet
- integrated services digital network (ISDN) line
- local area network (LAN)
- notebook, or laptop, computers
- task analysis
- fax machine
- ergonomics
- wide area network (WAN)
- voice mail
- wireless technology
- equal employment opportunity (EEO).

By now, you should have a fair idea of what telecommuting is, what it isn't, and what it may be. It is not as simple a concept as it first might appear when an employee asks to work from home. As one of my clients said after our first meeting on telecommuting, "This is complicated stuff!"

The next chapter explores why an organization might want to say yes or no to an employee's request to telecommute and how a company can decide if telecommuting is a feasible nontraditional work process.

# 2

# Why Organizations Choose Telecommuting

---

*"It makes me more productive to do things when they need to be done, and not just from 9 to 5."*

—Experienced Telecommuter

---

This chapter can help readers consider the implications of telecommuting for their organizations. So why would an organization want to consider telecommuting? There are about as many reasons as there are organizations, but there are a few general motives that are the most prevalent.

## Employee Satisfaction

Employee satisfaction is not really one result of telecommuting; it is, however, the outgrowth of several of telecommuting's effects. Telecommuters' effective control of time, ability to produce, and reduced stress together increase their satisfaction with work.

### Control of Time

On a basic level, telecommuting simply provides workers with the convenience of no longer having to commute to the office each day. Some surveys indicate that just over half of the employees asked give reduced commuting as their primary reason for telecommuting. (Descriptions of these and other studies cited in this chapter appear in some of the books listed in the suggested readings at the end of this book.) Government and private studies have indicated that the average commute for most workers almost doubled between 1960 and 1985, and this was only based on mileage, not on increased time because of traffic and road conditions. The aggregate amount of time spent in traffic, on buses and trains, even walking, just to get to work is mind boggling.

A worker with a 10-minute commute will spend 80 hours, or approximately two full workweeks, commuting each year. If that commute is 40 minutes each way, it is equivalent to about eight workweeks or 320 hours per year. Add to this the cost of gas, tolls, parking, and auto repair and replacement, and it is easy to see why the ability to telecommute for even a few days a month creates employees who are more satisfied with their jobs. Some studies report that about a quarter of the respondents cite reduced trans-portation expenses as their reason for telecommuting.

In most cases, commuting time is not compensated time or even personal time. The commute is really just another work task, at times a dangerous one, that requires intense concentration. About the best that I can say for a commute is that it provides a chance to listen to a good audio book tape during a traffic tie-up or wait for a bus. A commute is time away from family and from doing things people like to be doing. It is often the ultimate stress time of the day, no matter what the car manufactures' commercials would like us to believe about the peace and quiet in their vehicles.

Telecommuting provides employees with more control over their time. Medical and dental appointments, child-care schedules, even walking the dog are all less of a problem for telecommuters. Telecommuting provides greater control over working conditions, heat, sound, and other environmental factors. On a psychological level, telecommuting can allow employees to work at the time of day (or night) during which they are most creative, what is known as working to their biological clock.

## Productivity

These factors that increase employee satisfaction, and others we haven't yet mentioned, increase productivity as well. In fact, from an organization's point of view, employee satisfaction and productivity are so closely related that they can be said to be part of the same reason for considering a telecommuting intervention.

Organizations such as CDC and Aetna Life and Casuality have reported double digit gains in the productivity of telecommuters over their stay-in-the-office colleagues. Reports of 20, 30, and even 40 percent gains are not uncommon. One organization in Florida reported a 300 percent productivity gain when it instituted telecommuting. Of course, much of this growth depends on how companies calculate productivity and what they are comparing, but there is no doubt that 15 to 20 percent gains in productivity for the average telecommuter are not beyond the reach of any company that has a well-implemented telecommuting intervention.

Some reports on telecommuting report that telecommuters say the quantity and quality of their work have increased as a result of telecommuting and that their managers say there are measurable gains in productivity. (See suggested readings.) There are many reasons for these productivity gains, and they are closely related to increases in employee satisfaction. Some pessimists contend that because telecommuters don't spend time commuting and have their work always around, they tend to work more hours and thus are more productive. This may be true in some cases. Even so, if the employees are satisfied and prefer to work extra hours, is that a bad thing?

More optimistic observers note that telecommuting reduces the incidences of absenteeism. Pacific Bell and the State of California report 25 percent decreases in absenteeism among telecommuters.

## Stress

The final employee satisfaction issue related to telecommuting is probably the most obvious. Studies show that just over half of telecommuters surveyed reported that telecommuting had reduced their job-related stress. The reasons for the decline in stress vary with each telecommuter, but they include such diverse concepts as the workers' ability to do the following: choose their own office environment (heat, light, music, privacy); increase flexibility in child or elder care; spend more time with their family; concentrate when necessary, free from unwanted office interruptions; and increase flexibility in scheduling personal chores. In short, telecommuters simply are more in control of their life.

# Cost-Reduction Issues

A second class of reasons an organization might choose to consider telecommuting is related to the cost of doing business, especially real estate costs.

## Reduced Real Estate Costs

Administrators typically mention capital expenditures for real estate as a cost savings from telecommuting. Through telecommuting, companies can reduce their need for office space. In larger organizations with well-implemented telecommuting initiatives, companies can put entire buildings to a new use, buildings can be sold, or better yet, buildings need not be built.

## Reduced Operational Costs

Telecommuting also contributes to a decline in the need for companies to transfer employees to other sites using company funds. Because employees no longer have to be on-site to complete their work, companies may no longer have to move employees to a new location when changes occur in its structure or in customers' needs. This reduced need to relocate workers also affects employee satisfaction and employee stress. Numerous surveys list moving on the top 10 list of life's most stressful moments. It causes stress not only for people who don't want to move but also for those who agree to do so.

Telecommuting reduces the need to pay premium salaries to people in geographic areas where their skills are in great demand but the labor pool is small. It also decreases, or even eliminates, the need to pay bonuses to move workers to less desirable towns where their skills are needed.

## Government Regulations

A third class of reasons that may motivate a company to consider telecommuting is related to government regulations, particularly environmental ones.

It might be interesting, but not particularly useful, to list all of the federal, state, and local environmental laws, statutes, and advisories dealing with the environment that affect business and can, in turn, be affected by a telecommuting initiative. The most comprehensive are the Federal Clean Air Act of 1990 and the State of California's laws. Communities nationwide also have their own regulations. By the time this book is published, there will be many more, probably even more restrictive and demanding than the ones already in existence.

Our society has made the decision that something must be done about air pollution and its chief purveyor, the automobile. Mass transit has helped a bit in controlling pollution, as have appeals to people's good sense, but these initiatives have not done nearly enough. So the emphasis now seems to be moving toward making employers responsible for decreasing commuting, and therefore pollution. The Federal Clean Air Act of 1990 made this relatively clear by mandating that employers reduce their employees' solo commutes by car or face rather stiff penalties. State statutes like those in California and Connecticut put an even greater burden on employers to reduce commuting by employees.

Telecommuting is probably the most logical and effective approach to dealing with these regulations. It takes cars off the street, and that is what the regulations require.

Recently some of my clients have hung posters in employee areas that describe ozone pollution problems and how their employees can help reduce pollution at key times to safeguard the ozone layer. Perhaps if these companies had an effective telecommuting program, they would have no need for the posters because the ozone layer would likely not be in jeopardy from too much pollution in too concentrated a period of time (that is, the rush hour). What a great boon for everyone, and one that could even save the company money!

Telecommuting can also have an effect on other government regulations. The most extensive of these is the ADA. Companies that help those with disabilities to be fully functioning members of an organization in an office environment can find it extremely expensive and rather inefficient for both the employee and the company.

A telecommuting process, however, can meet employees' needs by allowing people with disabilities to work from home, where they are normally well equipped to handle living and working contingencies, and meet government regulations at the same time.

One word of caution is necessary. Such benefits can only accrue when an organization has established a well thought out and formalized telecommuting program. Having individuals simply work at home will not meet the criteria of acts such as the ADA. There are many disadvantages to telecommuting, a number of which can seriously affect an employee's career if they are not taken into account when the program is designed. These disadvantages must be reconciled through proper planning and implementation if a telecommuting intervention is to meet the ADA's mandates. Later chapters will cover planning in detail.

Another federal regulation that can be at least partially adhered to through the use of telecommuting is the Family and Medical Leave Act, which permits workers to take unpaid leave to deal with medical issues. An organization with a telecommuting program in place can more effectively react to the needs of employees who require leave for family reasons, yet still need to earn a salary or are an important part of the organization.

## The Community

Most companies are interested in being good corporate citizens in their communities. An organization's telecommuting intervention can affect the community in a number of ways. The first and most obvious way is the environmental impact, that is, cleaner air. Additionally, less commuting, and therefore less traffic also means reduced energy usage, decreased congestion for those that must commute, and fewer road repairs, which can be a huge cost savings for strapped municipal budgets. Telecommuting can also take the pressure off crowded public transportation facilities, not to mention the possibility of reducing traffic fatalities. With fewer commuters, there will be less need for expensive buses and trains and a decrease in the ancillary costs associated with them.

On a more esoteric plane, with the reduction in cars downtown, cities can use the money they are saving to turn lifeless concrete parking lots into parks and green spaces. This reversal of singer Joni Mitchell's lament of "Taking Paradise and putting up a parking lot" from the song "Big Yellow Taxi" isn't beyond the realm of possibility with telecommuting. Even discussing these issues is great for an organization's community image and the public relations that are an integral part of that image.

## Summary of Telecommuting Advantages

Following is a summary of the telecommuting advantages, including some not yet mentioned, beginning with the possible advantages of a telecommuting initiative for companies:

- **Geographic labor shortages:** Telecommuters are not geographically dependent.

- **Retention:** Because of companies' reduced need to relocate employees, and the dissatisfaction that creates, telecommuting can reduce turnover.
- **Recruitment:** Organizations with a telecommuting program have a big advantage over those that don't have one.
- **ADA:** Telecommuting can make employment of workers with disabilities a win-win situation from every point of view.
- **Environmental regulations:** Telecommuting is the most effective and advantageous way to deal with the mandates of these laws.
- **Sick time:** Employees working at home call in sick less often on both telecommuting and office days, work when they are a little under the weather because they don't need to face a commute or the office, and take fewer sick days for problems not related to illnesses.
- **Absenteeism due to family crisis:** Telecommuters have the flexibility to handle big and small family problems without missing work.
- **Productivity increases:** Productivity is higher for telecommuters than for their colleagues in offices.
- **Job satisfaction:** Workers who are correctly chosen to be telecommuters have increased satisfaction.
- **Employee safety issues:** Homes are safer than cars, and safer than offices too.
- **Disaster mitigation:** Hurricanes, earthquakes, even fires that shut down company offices do not necessarily shut down the telecommuter.
- **Reduced overtime:** The productivity gains of telecommuting alone reduce overtime costs.
- **Better customer service during off-peak hours:** Larger companies with many telecommuters can staff call centers 24 hours a day by people who never leave their homes.
- **Fewer moves:** This is an advantage for the organization, the telecommuter, even the community because people stay in one place longer.

- **Better space utilization:** When telecommuting programs are well planned, companies can make good use of their space. If the planning and implementation is haphazard, however, an organization will end up with groups of people who simply have two offices instead of one.

Following are some of the advantages of telecommuting for individual employees:

- **Work at home:** Work at home means different things to different people, but in most cases, who wouldn't want to? (Employees who wouldn't want to work at home make poor telecommuters and should never be forced into the home environment. A good first question to ask when choosing telecommuters is, Do you want to work at home?)
- **Privacy:** Gone are cubicles that let in noise, lead to distractions, and enable passersby to see whatever's on the desk.
- **Work when most productive:** Telecommuters don't have to work the same hours as those in their main office. Some people (I confess to being one of them) are most productive after their afternoon nap.
- **Reduced transportation costs and commuting time:** Depending on the commute, telecommuters can save hundreds and even thousands of dollars a year. Some people report that working from home is like getting a raise that costs the company nothing.
- **Reduced clothing costs:** The clothes most people wear around the house are not normally as expensive as the ones they wear to work, and replacing them isn't as expensive either.
- **Reduced stress:** For starters, no car, no traffic, less stress.
- **Expansion of the geographic job-opportunity base:** Telecommuters can apply for a job in any part of a company without considering geographic restrictions. Expansion of the geographic base is an advantage for job hunters as well, and so falls under a company's recruitment aspect mentioned earlier.

- **Control of furnishings:** For some people this can be as simple as a stool to put up their feet, for others as complicated as lights that don't hurt their eyes, but telecommuting allows for this and much more.
- **Control of environment:** Telecommuters seldom face the problem of freezing in the winter in poorly planned office environments or fighting with their office mates over the thermostat setting. And, if they concentrate better with a Mozart symphony playing at the stereo's top decibel level, no one is there to complain (except possibly the neighbors if they happen to be telecommuters, too).
- **Lunch schedules and prices:** You can have lunch whenever you want, whether it's noon, 1:30 p.m., or 11 a.m. As for price, telecommuters seldom get tempted to go to lunch at an expensive new restaurant. On a negative note, the amount of business (and important gossip) that takes place over lunch can be amazing and critical. The telecommuter must find ways to substitute for lunches not attended.
- **Less need to relocate for a better position in the company:** It doesn't matter where telecommuters are based if their jobs can be performed at home.
- **End to office drop ins:** "Hey, have you got a minute?" A request seldom heard, and an interruption not often missed, in a telecommuting environment.
- **Elimination of unplanned and unproductive meetings:** Meetings that begin with "Hey, have you got a minute" and have no productive outcome basically disappear in a telecommuting environment.
- **More flexible child care:** Although telecommuting is not a substitute for child care, it can make child care easier by allowing the telecommuter more flexible schedules.
- **More flexible elder care:** Their flexible schedules enable telecommuters more leeway in making elder-care arrangements, a growing concern in our society.

- **Fresh start each day:** With a commute from the bedroom to the office down the hall, telecommuters get to work feeling refreshed, particularly if they grabbed a nice fresh cup of coffee while traversing the traffic in the kitchen.
- **Fewer phone interruptions:** Because the telecommuter is not in the same location as other workers, in-office colleagues seem to have a psychological aversion to calling the at-home worker unless it's important. Although this mindset reduces unnecessary interruptions, it can become a negative if the impression becomes out of "site," out of mind.
- **Personal chores:** Under planned and authorized circumstances, the telecommuter's banking, doctors' appointments, scheduling of repair people, and other personal necessities can be taken care of when most other people are at work and not trying to get them done.
- **Better communications:** Telecommuters who are involved in well-designed programs report that they actually communicate more often and effectively with their supervisor and others in the company than they did when they were in the office every day.
- **Family time:** The saving in time commuting is a family-time bonus for telecommuters. Surveys show that telecommuters report more satisfaction with their home life.
- **Information highway:** Many people are wary of the new technologies, the Internet, and other aspects of the information revolution. Telecommuters report that they quickly grow comfortable with these technologies in a way that they might never had otherwise.

These advantages affect the community in general:
- **Environmental impact:** Fewer cars cause less pollution.
- **Energy conservation:** Fewer cars mean less gas used.
- **Decreased traffic congestion:** Fewer cars cause less traffic.
- **Reduced road repair:** Fewer cars mean less wear and tear on roads.

- **Public transportation:** Fewer cars reduce the pressure on public transportation. This decrease can have a negative side in that people will be less willing to support the concept of public transportation if it is underutilized.
- **Parking lots to parks:** With the reduced traffic, parking lots may give way to parks. (It be a dream, but perhaps it can come true.)
- **Reduction in neighborhood crime:** Many suburban neighborhoods become virtual ghost towns during the workday with both parents at work and the kids at school. This emptiness makes it much easier for thieves to work. Telecommuters are not police, but by their mere presence they send a signal that someone may be watching.

The categories are not totally discrete because a number of advantages flow into one another. Telecommuting is a highly relational process, with much of it being good for everyone involved.

## Summary of Telecommuting Disadvantages

The advantages of telecommuting can be a double-edged sword. For example, the cost reduction from eliminating the need to construct buildings can be an advantage for companies that employ telecommuters. It can also be a disadvantage for construction workers and the companies that employ them. Other advantages of telecommuting can also create disadvantages because of the need for fewer road workers, parking attendants, bus drivers, and other employees. Even something as beneficial as a telecommuter's control over his or her own work environment has a down side in that the telecommuter normally pays for the electricity and heat (few programs reimburse employees for these aspects).

Fortunately, most of the disadvantages of telecommuting can be eliminated or at least considerably reduced by initiating a program that has been well planned and properly implemented. Most of the rest of this book will deal with doing just that. But before we start on this not inconsiderable task, here is a list of those disadvantages, starting with those for companies:

- **Loss of control:** Does anyone really know what those telecommuters are doing? If a telecommuting program is well devised and administrated, the answer can be yes, and maybe it doesn't even matter.
- **Decrease in supervision:** Not being able to physically see their supervisees every day makes some supervisors nervous, particularly those who aren't very effective. Telecommuting can reduce supervisory effectiveness if it's already done badly, but it actually increases supervision that's done well.
- **Employee abuse:** Some employees will abuse telecommuting. Some also abuse their lunch break, the lack of time clocks, and just about anything else they can. The important point is that telecommuting is a process of trust. Employers who don't trust employees not to abuse telecommuting shouldn't undertake it. And employers should handle those that abuse the trust as they would any employee who takes too many liberties with a system. However, put the blame on the employee where it rightfully belongs, not on the telecommuting process.
- **Decreased flexibility for the unplanned:** For companies where crisis is a normal procedure, the loss of flexibility is a big disadvantage. It becomes difficult to bring the entire staff together for an emergency meeting if most of them are at home. If crisis is your business's way for life, telecommuting may not be for you.
- **Mechanical problems:** These can be as simple as running out of paper or as complex as a computer crash. Whatever it is, the people who can fix it are seldom hanging around the telecommuter's house, and it may be a day or two before they can get there.
- **Greater coordination needs:** Knowing things like the hours employees will be at their desk, the days they'll be in the

office, and even how the work is progressing are more difficult in a telecommuting environment. Mechanisms and tools must be set up so that everyone stays in contact and knows one another's moves.

- **Loss of communication between the telecommuter and office:** A problem in a poorly devised telecommuting process can become an advantage in a good program.
- **Suitability to only certain jobs:** Telecommuting isn't effective for every job. One of the first things a business needs to consider when thinking about telecommuting is which jobs it will work for. We'll discuss this in the next chapter.

Following are some disadvantages for telecommuters:

- **Work at home:** One of the biggest personal advantages is also one of the disadvantages for reasons that follow.
- **Loneliness and isolation:** People who spend almost all their time telecommuting find that loneliness and isolation can be a big problem. They can also be a detriment for gregarious people who like the give and take of personal communications in the office environment. An important reason for choosing telecommuters wisely is that not all people can take these problems.
- **Cabin fever:** If you work where you live, and live where you work, you can often go for days without leaving the house. Some people like this. It makes the rest of us (even good telecommuters) crazy if we let it go on too long.
- **Lack of respect or jealousy from colleagues:** One of the disadvantages listed for a company was loss of control: Does anyone really know what those telecommuters are doing? Some people truly feel that telecommuters are probably not working when they are at home. Others simply would like to telecommute but can't because of the nature of their jobs. Some of these perceptions result from jealousy. They must be dealt with, or they'll bring down even the best telecommuting program.

- **Loss of communications:** This disadvantage from the organization's point of view can also be a personal disadvantage if the telecommuter is kept out of conversations (both formal and informal) that are important to the work processes.
- **Workaholism:** There is little question that many telecommuters work longer days than their in-office colleagues. When it goes to extremes, it is termed workaholism and can be just as detrimental to the health of the telecommuter as any other psychological malady.
- **Family distractions:** Family schedules seldom follow those of the telecommuter perfectly. Kids come home from school, spouses are off on a day the telecommuter is not, someone is sick, and so forth. Discipline on the part of the telecommuter is necessary to keep family distractions to a minimum during work hours. Not everyone can find such discipline within himself or herself.
- **Loss of social interactions:** Studies seem to indicate that young unmarried people find most of their dates at the office, and a large percentage of people meet their spouses there. Telecommuters can lose a large portion of this important social ability. Also, it's difficult to stop after work for a drink with the gang if you are already home.
- **Loss of access to copiers, fax, and other office services:** Even the best-equipped home office seldom has all the equipment or services of a business center. Depending on the job, this might be a deciding factor against telecommuting in general. Sooner or later, it is at least a temporary minor inconvenience for anyone who telecommutes.
- **Invisibility:** In a poorly organized telecommuting environment, telecommuting can lead to out of "site," out of mind. It can be a huge detriment to promotion and the assignment of more interesting tasks, and it may even mark a telecommuter as an easy candidate for staff reduction. Even in the best

telecommuting program, both the telecommuter and management must guard against invisibility every day.

- **Job path displacement:** Closely related to invisibility, this disadvantage occurs when telecommuters do not receive tasks that would develop them for the next highest position. Supervisors may choose someone else because the telecommuters won't be around to ask questions or get the help they need on the tasks, or supervisors simply may have forgotten about the telecommuter because he or she isn't there.

- **Fast track:** Fast trackers in most companies are employees who work lots of hours and are seen doing all the right things at the right places. Telecommuters might work lots of hours, but who notices if their car is not still in the lot long after everyone else is gone? Telecommuters have a hard time maintaining a fast-track representation, except in those companies where accomplishment is more important than appearances.

- **Mail:** Basically, it's hard for telecommuters to send and get their company mail. Even in the best programs, it arrives later than if they were at the work site. E-mail can solve this to some extent, but isn't totally effective.

- **Off the grapevine:** The unofficial communications that come across the grapevine can protect workers or help them get ahead. Telecommuters lose opportunities to stay in touch with it.

- **Neighborhood UPS drop off:** When your neighbors know you're home all day, you will be surprised at the number of strange requests you might receive. Neighbors need to be aware that you are working at home, not simply available.

- **Ever-present office:** Telecommuters never get away from the office. Having all your work right there and undone can often weigh on a telecommuter's mind, particularly if the telecommuter does nothing about it. This problem is related to workaholism, but less destructive.

- **Overeating and other bad habits:** Ready access to the refrigerator, soap operas only a room away, a yard that needs to be mowed—these are problems for telecommuters who easily succumb to temptation.
- **Homemaker first:** This is more of a problem for women as it is a holdover from previous cultures, but it can also be true for men. Spouses can't understand why if you're home all day you can't do the laundry, take the clothes to the cleaners, make an earlier dinner, and the like. When workers begin telecommuting, they and their spouses must decide on rules about the activities they can do when they are home.
- **Things left at the office:** This may be the biggest disadvantage of telecommuting, or at least the most irritating aspect. No matter how well telecommuters plan, they will find times when they need things they left at the office. If this happens too often, a telecommuter will either need to do better planning or reconsider if telecommuting is right for his or her particular job.

Communities really have few reactions to telecommuting that aren't beneficial. The items on the following list are a bit of a stretch:

- **Job and revenue losses:** Companies that have telecommuters do not bring the number of jobs to a community that the community anticipates. The community also loses ancillary jobs, like bus drivers, parking lot attendants, and home builders.
- **Reduced society mixing:** Telecommuting limits the cultural mixing of our society. Suburbanites stay in the suburbs and city dwellers stay in the city. I believe this is an even further reach than the job and revenue loss concept.

Basically, if telecommuting is done properly, it's good for the community, the business, and the telecommuter.

# 3

# Developing a Telecommuting Philosophy for an Organization

---

*"Well then, if it's that good, everyone will want to do it."*
—Experienced Telecommuter

---

This chapter will help readers determine if telecommuting will fit into their organization's philosophy and structure.

## Organizational Suitability

A lesson that business seems to have to relearn continuously is that every innovation that comes down the line is not suitable for every organization. This is true of management interventions such as total quality management, human resource innovations like self-managed teams, as well as organizational interventions like telecommuting that combine management, human resource, and technological changes.

In the past, companies that had little knowledge of telecommuting and even less of its suitability for them jumped on the bandwagon, announcing with great flourish that they had found a new way to save money and make employees happy. I call this approach the CEO Airline Magazine Syndrome (CAMS) because the impetus for it seems to come from the articles published in airline magazines, which bored CEOs read while flying from one meeting to another. A CEO mentions the article at a meeting, and someone gets the idea that this is a command rather than a comment. Soon, and with little real research or thought, everyone is convinced the answer to all the company's problems is telecommuting, or reengineering, or learning organizations, or some other fashionable idea.

CAMS, or any variation of it, is not a decision-making approach to use when considering telecommuting. An organization will be expending a great deal of resources to get a telecommuting process implemented, and it will be setting new and personal expectations for the workers involved. The decision-making process needs to be systematic and thorough.

## Why Consider Telecommuting?

This is the most basic question, yet one that is often not explored in enough detail. The reasons are usually evident—reduce real estate costs, increase employee satisfaction, possibly even increase productivity if the company's analysis of the concept has gone into some depth, but this question needs to be asked in much more detail than that.

The deeper questions are the following: What are the basic business drivers that caused the company to think about telecommuting in the first place? What does the company really hope to gain, not in vague generalities and concepts, but in specific end results. What is it willing to risk and do to institute telecommuting, and just as important, what is it not willing to do?

The lists in chapter 2 can help in an analysis of the advantages and disadvantages of telecommuting. They enumerate most of the possible reasons for considering telecommuting and can provide a structure for an analysis.

# The Telecommuting Committee

Readers might be asking, "Who does all this analysis?" Is it the human resources (HR) department, the real estate department, someone in administration, or perhaps the MIS department because telecommuting is a technological intervention? The answer is all of the above.

Although some organizations rely on a single person to do their telecommuting research and others gather information separately from various parts of the organization, the best way to do a telecommuting analysis is to establish a telecommuting committee made up of representatives from the departments that will be affected by it, or at least by the decision to go with it or not. The HR, real estate, administration, and MIS departments usually make up the core group for such a team, with other members being added as needs dictate.

People assigned to the telecommuting committee should have the expertise to answer any questions that will arise about their area and its relation to telecommuting, and they should have the experience and stature to make at least preliminary decisions on the telecommuting issues for their department.

These groups can function very well with or without a chosen leader, but they need a full-time secretary who is not one of the experts. The discussions will range far and wide with many ideas given and rejected, so the secretary must concentrate on what is being said and recorded, and not on how to answer a point about an area of expertise. For the purpose of this book, assume that a telecommuting committee undertakes the analysis.

## Is This Organization a Good Candidate for Telecommuting?

Now that the committee has a substantial idea of why it is considering telecommuting, its next task is to make sure its organization fits the telecommuting mold. There isn't much of a mold. In fact, it's pretty elastic, with different organizations having different approaches to telecommuting. There are a few questions the committee can ask about itself that are basic to just about any telecommuting process.

## Does This Company Have the Right Jobs for Telecommuting?

This is a basic question and one that requires careful consideration. Some jobs lend themselves to telecommuting, some do not, and some might if both the job and the telecommuting intervention were constructed carefully enough.

The best approach to deciding if a job is right for telecommuting is to look at the tasks that make up the job. If an organization has an efficient training department, many of the company's jobs have probably already been analyzed to determine the job tasks. Others may need analysis that can be done relatively quickly. The committee should let the training manager know that it needs a job analysis, not a task analysis. If the training manager does not know how the two differ, a training consultant might be a better resource for the job analysis. A company can save plenty of time and money by undertaking the correct analysis.

Some organizations make the mistake of thinking their job descriptions will give them what they need for this process. I've seen one or two that have the level of detail needed, but these are few and far between. Just as a company doesn't need the detail of a task analysis, it doesn't need more detail than most job descriptions provide.

Analyzing a job task list for telecommuting is easy enough. Simply ask, "Can this task be done efficiently in a home environment, or must it be done at the office?" The committee should try to be as objective as possible, or better yet, for each task, it should ask two or three job incumbents and possibly a supervisor.

It is easy to get really fancy with this analysis by describing the task applicability in terms of percentages (70 percent of the task can be done at home), or adding a criticality factor (this task can't be done at home, but it is not critical to the job), or by doing percentage sums (55 percent of the critical tasks and 80 percent of the non-critical tasks could be done in a home environment). However, in the end the analysis is subjective. The basis of the analysis remains the same no matter how many figures someone adds: Can the task be done at home, and are there enough at-home tasks to make it worthwhile to move this job into a telecommuting environment?

Other concepts to use when analyzing jobs for telecommuting suitability include the following:

- How much face-to-face time with other employees is required in the job?
- How often do job incumbents need to drop what they are doing to deal with emergency situations?
- What types of office resources that can't be found in a home environment (such as files, references, one of a kind material, and secure or sensitive material) does the job need access to, and how often?
- What types of special machines does the job need access to and how often?

If the committee or analyst responds "too often," the job is not suitable for telecommuting.

### Does This Company Have the Right People for Telecommuting?

Once the committee decides that the organization has enough jobs to justify a telecommuting program, it needs to determine if the job incumbents are capable of working in the telecommuting environment.

This process is individualistic and involves a number of factors, many of which appear in the subsequent chapters on telecommuter training. A more general process applies to this suitability analysis. The committee can use 10 basic characteristics of successful telecommuters to help in its determination. Although each member of the target telecommuter group does not need to have all of these characteristics, the group as a whole should have most of them, and in abundance.

The general telecommuter population should be the following:

- Self-motivated: They will have to provide their own motivation.
- Self-disciplined: No one is going to be there to watch their hours.
- Flexible: Things will be changing quickly, now and later.
- Socially mature: They don't need the office society to find dates and mates.
- Experienced in their jobs: Their networks are well-established, and they know the company.
- Skilled in their jobs: Telecommuting is a poor place for training.
- Comfortable with their family life: Telecommuting won't solve their family problems.
- Good at planning and managing their own time and work
- Good communicators: Communications will be more difficult.
- Employees who work for results, not just to put in hours.

### Is Our Company Willing to Support Telecommuting?

This question may seem superfluous, but it isn't. Telecommuting is not an intervention that a company just starts and then ignores. It requires the organization's continual support if it is to flourish. For a company to get the full benefit from telecommuting, it needs a mechanism for continuing support and evaluation of the intervention. In many of the most successful implementations, the organization has created a position of telecommuting ombudsman to oversee the process in operation and to deal with the telecommuters' or their supervisors' issues or those of anyone else involved.

In other situations, a reduced version of the telecommuting committee has been charged with meeting periodically to evaluate the progress of the intervention. A company may choose either of these methods, or something else that fits it better.

### Are the Supervisors Able to Accept Telecommuting?

This question is often overlooked, much to the dismay of some organizations when it comes time to train their supervisors for telecommuting. The telecommuter's supervisor is an integral part of the telecommuting process and can easily make or break the entire intervention. If a company's management style is not flexible or supportive, then the supervisors will not have the necessary characteristics to supervise telecommuters. In fact, they will probably do whatever they can to keep their employees from becoming telecommuters.

The supervisors are not really at fault if they've been trained to supervise with high levels of control and the need to know what is happening all the time. For example, a management style that depends on walking around will not be particularly effective if walking around means going from house to house to see what's happening.

As part of a suitability analysis, the committee must decide if its management philosophy, and the way its supervisors interpret it, is suitable to telecommuting. Will they be flexible enough to deal with a telecommuter's particular needs? Can they communicate effectively with people they don't see very often? Can they handle the idea that people will be working at home, away from their immediate control and availability? Basically, can they change their supervisory style to match the needs of telecommuting?

If the answer to that last question is no, the committee has two choices. The first is to retrain its supervisors on basic supervisory principles, which will take a lot of resources and still may not be effective. The second is to seriously reconsider its company's suitability for telecommuting. Chapter 8 describes the training of supervisors for the purpose of augmenting the competencies and beliefs they already have. If the supervisors do not have the right mindset for telecommuting at the beginning, it is doubtful that the intervention will succeed even with training.

## Are the Benefits Worth the Effort?

This question is an overall final check of the organization's telecommuting candidacy. A committee that has reached this point knows that it has the right jobs, the right people, and the support. Now it must ask itself if in the long run (and the short run too, for that matter) telecommuting will be worth it? There will be expenses, dislocations, lost productivity for a time, probably some jealousy, likely a few failures, and other problems that the committee can't foresee. The committee should take another look at why it wants to begin a telecommuting intervention, review the resources at its disposal, make the final decision, and then go for it!

## Defining Telecommuting for the Organization

With the preliminary analysis done and a decision to continue made, the next step in implementing a telecommuting intervention is to develop the organization's telecommuting philosophy. The first step in this process is to define telecommuting for the organization. This task actually began in the suitability analysis when the committee was determining why it was considering telecommuting. This determination should be reflected in its definition.

A number of definitions of telecommuting appeared in chapter 1, and these reflected some varying concepts of the process. To solidify a company's own definition, the committee should ask such questions as the following: Will telecommuting be strictly an at-home process, or will it provide workers with telecommuting centers? Will virtual offices be part of the telecommuting intervention? Will the company use hoteling? Will there be team spacing, shared spaces, compressed workweeks, or job sharing?

The definition should clearly state what telecommuting will and won't be for the organization. Depending on an organization's concept, it could choose a definition like one of the following:

- We define *telecommuting* as moving our employees from the office to their homes and supplying them with the technology and support to do their work in the home environment.
- We define *telecommuting* as any process in which work is not done in the assigned office environment.
- We define *telecommuting* as a combination of flextime and flexiplace that allows our employees to work where they want and when they want to be their most productive.

These are examples of various companies' definitions of telecommuting. The first is specific, the second general, and the third brings in aspects that go beyond what might be considered basic telecommuting. All of these, and anything else the committee wishes to say, can be part of the definition, but remember that it is the definition that will guide what the company does and doesn't do later, and what the telecommuters expect from the program. So the committee should make it specific enough to be useful and understandable for everyone.

When considering the definition, the committee may want to use a telecommuting model. There are a number of these, but they are usually variations on one of four basic types:

- In the *departmental model,* one or two areas of the company, such as the call center or data entry, are singled out for telecommuting. This model provides only a few of the advantages of companywide telecommuting and has a number of built-in disadvantages.

- In the *corporate-wide model,* large areas of the company or the entire company participates in telecommuting, according to certain eligibility criteria for the telecommuter. (This book concentrates primarily on this model.)

- The *individual model* is one in which an employee and his or her supervisor make their own telecommuting arrangements with the company's blessing but little formal support. The company loses some major advantages in this model, but it is cheaper and easier to run than the departmental and corporate-wide methods.

- In the *contractor model,* employees are moved out of the office and paid as if they were independent contractors working from their homes. This model is extremely cost-effective, but many people consider it unfair to the employees, and that sentiment tends to decrease moral and company loyalty. The government also examines these arrangements scrupulously to ensure that the workers are independent contractors and not employees. I do not recommend this model at all, unless your company enjoys spending a lot of time in court.

# A Telecommuting Vision

With a definition in hand, the committee can now develop the central core of its telecommuting philosophy, the company's telecommuting vision. The vision is primarily a statement of the company's philosophy. It explains to everyone who is interested why the company is attempting this intervention and what it will accomplish. It doesn't necessarily have to be long or involved, but it should cover these important points:

- *Why is the company doing this?* What does the company see as achievable benefits for it, the employees, and the community? The committee can use its analysis and the advantages list from chapter 2 to finalize this statement.
- *Who will be telecommuting?* The committee laid the groundwork for this aspect of the vision in its analysis of jobs and people. The statement should start with a targetcd goal of how many telecommuters it hopes to have when the process is fully implemented. Some companies give a range of the minimum and maximum numbers. The statement should include which departments will be eligible to participate in the telecommuting initiative, which job classifications, and how many people from any department or job, or if it is simpler, the statement could say who is not eligible. Any other stipulations concerning participation should also go here. If telecommuting implementation will be in stages, its schedule should go here.
- The final aspect of your vision should answer *when*. Specifically, it should say when the first telecommuter will start, when full implementation will be achieved, and any other important time frames.

The reasons for each decision also belong in the vision document. The "why" of each vision is just as important as the "what" and will help to guide the ombudsman, supervisors, telecommuting committee, or anyone else who develops and administers the intervention.

# Costs

It might seem surprising that cost has anything to do with a telecommuting philosophy, but I've found from sad experience that it has much to do with it. If an organization has gotten through the definition and vision pieces, it may be feeling pretty good. An estimate of the cost can quickly transform the mood to one of mean reality. It may show that it is not feasible for the company to implement telecommuting, and if that's the case, it is better to realize that early.

There are three major cost areas in telecommuting: technology costs, training costs, and continued costs. Because this is a philosophy and not a business plan, exact costs are not under consideration. Those will come later in this book with descriptions of the development of specific telecommuting policies and procedures. Approximations can now help the committee decide if the company can fiscally support the intervention it outlined in its vision.

## Technology Costs

Technology costs are those associated with setting up the program. They include pure technology costs such as the price of computers, other hardware, networks, and software. At this time, the committee will begin to make preliminary decisions about how to equip telecommuters, what they will have and won't be able to have in their home environment, and how they will be set up with the main office. These decisions will change as the committee creates its policies and procedures and undertakes more research. It is advisable to consider the technological aspect early because staff will be asking questions about equipment as soon as it hears that the company is looking into telecommuting.

More information about technology appears in the next chapter, but the goal here is to figure an approximate technology cost for the intervention. Along with technology costs, it is useful to assess any other start-up costs for the program. The costs might be as simple as those for publicizing the new initiative or as complex as those for the safety inspectors who will check each telecommuter's house for wiring deficits before installing the equipment. In some telecommuting processes, these miscellaneous costs are so much smaller than the technology costs that they are quite properly ignored, but in other interventions, they can be significant. It is important to consider these costs carefully before proceeding.

## Training Costs

The second major cost area for telecommuting is training costs. Training costs come in two categories, direct and indirect costs. Direct costs are those that people usually think of when they consider training, such as the cost of developing a training program (in the case of telecommuting, at least three programs), materials, rooms and materials for teaching, trainer travel, and record keeping.

Indirect costs are mostly associated with productive time lost while employees are away from their jobs learning about telecommuting. Participants' travel costs to the telecommuting program are also indirect costs. Indirect costs can be quite high because nearly all employees will need training, including managers, supervisors, telecommuters, and even people in the telecommuting departments who don't telecommute.

If the number one cause of failure of a telecommuting intervention is not doing careful planning, a close second is not training everyone who needs to be trained to implement it. The committee should decide who and how many and what the basic costs (both direct and indirect) will be.

## Continued Costs

The third cost area, continued costs, is the cost of the continued support of the telecommuting process. Technology support is the main item. If equipment breaks down at a telecommuter's home, how much is it going to cost to fix it. Phone bills, networking bills, costs of network upkeep, and upgrading at remote sites are also possible costs. These estimates require careful research because many of them may be normal company costs whether a telecommuting process is going on or not. Normal company costs can be ignored, or at least discounted. The critical element in this assessment is the cost difference between doing these things as the company has been and doing them in a telecommuting environment.

### The Final Estimate

To complete the cost estimate for the telecommuting philosophy, the committee should prepare an amortization schedule for the first two cost aspects. Chances are the organization is implementing a telecommuting program to save money or to increase productivity, or to do both. The schedule will show how long it will take to amortize the start-up costs based on the estimate of cost savings. Because cost savings should continue, it might be possible to write off some of the continued costs against them.

The appraising, estimating, and calculating should provide figures for what it will cost to begin the telecommuting intervention, what the continuing costs will be, and when the cost savings will begin. These three figures go into the vision statement, and the rest of the work will be useful later.

Just a note of caution: If one of the main justifications for telecommuting was cost savings, but it doesn't show up here or will take years to happen, the committee may want to rethink the whole idea of telecommuting.

## Policies and Procedures

The policies and procedures that an organization implements to make telecommuting work are the final part of a telecommuting philosophy. However, policies and procedures are a relatively complex process that more or less straddles the line between philosophy and implementation. The next chapter covers the process in some detail.

# Summary of Key Concepts

Following is a summary checklist of the key concepts of an organizational analysis that committees can use:

- [ ] Why are we considering implementing a telecommuting program?
- [ ] Do we have jobs that are applicable to telecommuting?
- [ ] Do we have people who will be good telecommuters?
- [ ] Can we support continued telecommuting?
- [ ] Will our supervisors function well in a telecommuting environment?
- [ ] What is our company's definition of telecommuting?
- [ ] What is our telecommuting vision?
  - How does the company benefit?
  - How do our employees benefit?
  - How might the community benefit?
  - What is a target number of telecommuters?
  - What will our estimated costs be—technology, training, and continued?
  - How long before we might see actual cost savings?

# 4

# Organizational Policies and Procedures Needed for Telecommuting

---

*"What do I need most? Clearer policies and procedures!*
*Oh, and a more comfortable chair."*

—Experienced Telecommuter

---

To achieve their organizational vision and goals and administer the telecommuting process, companies need carefully designed policies and procedures. This chapter provides information about those policies and procedures to help companies develop theirs properly.

Policies and procedures make the vision of telecommuting a reality. Companies may give the responsibility for writing to someone on the telecommuting committee, to a different program implementer, or even to a skilled writer. Whoever writes the policies and procedures should consult with people intimately involved with the project, like the ombudsman whose function is to interpret policies and procedures. Good policies and procedures won't ensure that companies have a smooth running or even a successful telecommuting program, but companies with badly conceived or poorly written policies or procedures, or with none at all, have a pretty fair guarantee that their program will fail.

## Policies and Procedures Categories

For convenience it is useful to put telecommuting policies and procedures into four categories: telecommuting specific, technological, human resource development (HRD) related, and financial. Some policies and procedures fall into more than one category. These categories are only for convenience and to be serviceable in companies.

### Telecommuting Specific

Policies and procedures that are specific to the telecommuting environment make up the largest category. More than likely they will be new and will have to be written from scratch. The process probably will take a lot of research and time because it's unlikely that a company has a telecommuting expert on staff who can just sit down and write the policies and procedures; however, the process is unlikely to go through the typical rewriting, review, re-rewriting, re-reviewing, and basic hand-wringing cycle that regularly occurs during changes in an organization's procedures.

#### ELIGIBILITY

Fortunately, the telecommuting committee did basic planning for some of these policies and procedures when it wrote the telecommuting philosophy. For example, one of the policies the company will need pertains to eligibility for telecommuting. The committee gave this concept a lot of preliminary thought while formulating the vision. It now needs to finalize those thoughts and structure them on paper.

The telecommuting eligibility policy should include most if not all of the following:

- which departments, work groups, job classifications, or positions will be permitted or possibly required to participate in the telecommuting program
- the number of participants planned for, and if there is a maximum (or minimum) number from each group

- schedules regarding who will go first, second, last, or the like
- a statement about how telecommuting candidates will be chosen or, even better, a list of selection criteria.

The last item is particularly important because the committee should be careful to avoid raising expectations only to dash them later. Time with the company, time in the job, and performance appraisal ratings are examples of common quantitative selection criteria.

This section is a good place to describe some of the personal disadvantages of telecommuting that appeared in chapter 2 and to make employees aware that those who may fall into these categories will not be considered for the program. It is also the place to describe any formal testing or screening of candidates and the use of any instrumentation to determine telecommuting suitability.

A telecommuting application is often part of the eligibility process and procedure. Although it isn't a necessity, in larger programs it helps keep track of candidates and begins the winnowing-out process. The application may be a simple one-page document that asks for specific biographical data, or it may include small self-assessments based on what the committee determines telecommuters' behavioral characteristics should be. I've even seen applications that ask employees for an evaluation of their manager's characteristics as related to telecommuting.

More complex applications may ask for information on work space and equipment as well as information about how to contact the candidate, such as phone number and address. The document may be detailed so the company can use it as a basic telecommuting personnel record.

Some of the policies mentioned above require employees' participation and give a minimum number or participants. Telecommuting specialists disagree about the value of these policies. Telecommuting programs are not as effective if employees are required to participate, but in many situations, companies will not get the maximum or even the hoped-for benefit from the intervention if too few employees participate. I have no answer to this quandary except to say that in my experience if the telecommuting system is well planned and well implemented, employees will volunteer, and required participation will become a moot point.

## The Telecommuting Contract

This document is for use after an employee has been chosen for telecommuting and before he or she receives in-depth training. It outlines the duties and responsibilities of the employee, the supervisor, and the organization in the telecommuting environment. It usually refers to the policies and procedures for specifics, but it normally states in general terms items such as record-keeping needs, responsibility for company equipment, data security, minimum and maximum telecommuting hours, supervisory arrangements, travel time arrangements, and general scheduling.

Contracts may be as short as one page or as long as six. I've even seen agreements for supervisors that lay out their obligations if they choose to take on the responsibility of supervising telecommuters. I think this is a great idea and highly recommend it.

What telecommuting contracts have in common is a place for signatures, which makes things a bit more complicated. By requiring signatures, the document could legally be considered an employment document, certainly an HR document, and maybe other things the company did not intend. This legality shouldn't scare the company or stop it from using the form. The company should just be sure that whatever is in the telecommuting contract is congruent with its general policies and procedures and that the HR and legal departments carefully review the document. Some examples of telecommuting contracts are available in chapter 7.

## Telecommuting Committee

This group of policies and procedures deals with the oversight processes for a telecommuting initiative. Chapter 3 said the best way to do a telecommuting analysis is to establish a telecommuting committee made up of representatives from the departments that will be affected by it, or at least by the decision to go with it or not. Now is the time to formalize any ad hoc telecommuting committee. What is its charge? What will be its duration? What are its powers? Will it administrate, evaluate? Who will be on it and for how long?

Some telecommuting interventions start with a committee, but reduce it over time to a single person. If this is a company's plan, that person will need a job description and some administrative detail.

## TRAINING

Although this topic will be reviewed in detail in later chapters, its policy and procedure aspects need to be noted here. Basically policy statements should clarify who will be trained, and procedure statements should describe how. Questions to deal with include:

- Who will be invited to the telecommuting orientation, and what will they learn?
- How will candidates be chosen? (Notice that this relates to the eligibility policies and procedures.)
- What instrumentation will be used, and how will it be evaluated?
- When will telecommuting candidates officially be considered telecommuters?
- What training will be given only to those chosen to be telecommuters?
- What training will all managers and supervisors receive?
- What training will telecommuter supervisors receive?
- What training will be given to those in a telecommuting work group who are not telecommuting?

The training department or telecommuting consultants can help fill in details, but it is not necessary to have entire lesson plans and behavioral objectives in the policies and procedures. However, concise statements that reflect the training concept and plans in enough detail to guide trainers as they prepare their program are an important aspect of the telecommuting policies and procedures.

## MONITORING

Monitoring is one of the areas that organizations most often overlook when they are setting out their telecommuting policies and procedures. Telecommuting is not a start-it-and-forget-it type of intervention. It requires continuous feedback both up and down the organizational structure.

To ensure that a system is running efficiently, the people responsible for it need to monitor all aspects of it. It is necessary to plan the monitoring procedure early for it to be effective. The policy statement should say what will be monitored and by whom. The process should incorporate perspectives of supervisors, telecommuters, and those who are not telecommuting. The procedures need to indicate how the monitoring will occur and how often.

Interview checklists are one of the most effective monitoring tools for telecommuting. These lists can be developed for all elements or groups and administered either in person, by mail, or electronically. The normal fare includes general questions about how the system is working and what problems are occurring. However, this is a good tool for use in asking specific questions as well, particularly if there is any negative feedback through the grapevine or other monitoring processes, and to request ideas for improving the system. Those who are actually working within the telecommuting system will have insights other people may have missed. It may also be helpful to monitor management's response to the telecommuting initiative. Normally this step is short and general, often no more than a brief phone call to various individuals. The purpose is both to gain information data and keep top management involved in the process and aware of how it is working.

I can't stress enough how important this continual monitoring is. Telecommuting is a living process within an organization. It will go through growth spurts and periods of dormancy. It will wither and die if not well tended and occasionally fed and watered. Systematic monitoring is the only method available to discern how the initiative is faring and what forms of intervention it may need to keep it alive and healthy. Monitoring policies and procedures carefully and assigning people to the task who are committed to making it work are the best ways to accomplish this.

### EVALUATION

Evaluation plans are closely related to those for monitoring, but they have their own policies and procedures. The last chapter of this book looks at evaluation (and monitoring) in detail. The telecommuting policies and procedures should state how the company plans to evaluate the success of the intervention, particularly if the process is going to require input and time from participants (which it will).

Like monitoring, the evaluation policy should state what will be evaluated and by whom. It is useful to include a "why" statement to ensure that everybody is clear about the purpose of this evaluation. Procedures look at how and when.

Items relevant to evaluation include the following:

- productivity of telecommuters
- telecommuter performance (possibly compared to that of nontelecommuters)
- how the practice of telecommuting in the organization relates to the vision
- how satisfied the telecommuters and their supervisors are
- if the stated goals have been reached
- if the expected advantages have been realized
- if the cost savings have been realized.

### MOVING OUT/MOVING IN

This last group of policies and procedures for telecommuting specific is a catch-all, but it is related to how the telecommuter begins telecommuting. It includes policy on who decides when it is time to begin telecommuting (moving out) and procedures on how the transfer will take place (moving in). It details responsibilities for these processes, not only for the telecommuter and supervisor, but also for other departments, such as communications, MIS, HR, corporate safety, and real estate, that will have a hand in the move.

The procedures should include a checklist of what needs to be done and when for the supervisor, the telecommuter, and the other interested parties. Contact numbers and names, methods of communication, and necessary forms are all part of this process.

This might also be a good place to include policy and procedures concerning office space. As stated in chapter 2, one of the main advantages of telecommuting is reduced real estate costs, but companies that are not careful may end up with employees who simply have two offices instead of one.

It was also noted in an earlier chapter that telecommuters need to have some office days. This section is the place in which to practice cost control by selecting where they will sit on those days. These policies and procedures can take on almost any aspect, from a simple guideline on the number of telecommuters for each shared office space to a centrally administered office area that is tightly controlled and scheduled. If left to their own devices, supervisors will find "good" reasons why each of their telecommuters needs his or her own office for the in-office day. The policies and procedures in this area will keep this from happening and will maximize the real estate cost savings from telecommuting.

Any other miscellaneous policies and procedures that don't seem to fit elsewhere will probably be at home here.

## Technology

This category of policies and procedures deals with what telecommuters will need to create their home offices. Some elements in this category appear elsewhere as well. Although that overlap makes the development of policies and procedures a bit more confusing, it exemplifies how telecommuting interrelates to so much of what happens in the organization.

## Work Space

These policies and procedures deal with setting up the home office environment. Policy and procedures statements should deal with items such as:

- the minimum size needed for a home work space
- privacy requirements
- furniture the telecommuter is expected to provide
- furniture the company will provide
- responsibilities for upkeep and return of company furniture
- responsibility for changes or improvements to the work space, both original and ongoing, if they are deemed necessary
- responsibility for utilities and other ongoing costs
- policy regarding the use of outside couriers (FedEx, UPS, and the like) for both normal and emergency situations
- handling of corporate mail in both directions
- responsibility for necessary repairs and maintenance
- insurance requirements
- inspections.

Inspections are extremely important to spell out. Many companies require a safety inspection of the home office environment before they will approve it for telecommuting. Others require periodic inspections of their equipment. Some companies consider this an intrusion on their privacy. By making the policy clear early, companies will save possible problems later.

A clearly stated policy is important for companies that charge telecommuters for the safety inspection or require employees to pay for independent electrical inspections. By the way, I don't consider either of these practices fair or conducive to a good telecommuting environment, so now that I mentioned them, I'd ask that you please not emulate them.

A note of caution: In a telecommuting application, companies may have set out minimum requirements for space, privacy and furniture, and even basic technology. These requirements should be congruent with the ones listed here. This is one of those policy over-laps that can create confusion if companies are not careful.

In their policies and procedures, some companies provide detailed plans with diagrams, lists, and helpful hints for setting up the work space. Although this information would be useful and it is an excellent idea, it belongs more in the training portion of the pro-gram and not in policies and procedures.

## HARDWARE AND SUPPLIES

This is the area that most people think about when considering policies and procedures for telecommuting. Some of the policies and procedures that belong here are

- what computers will be used
- how network connections will be made
- what software will be necessary
- whether phones will be provided and what kind and how many
- whether special phone services such as call waiting, distinc-tive ringing, three-way calling, caller ID, or ISDN lines will be provided
- whether specialized phones such as cordless phones, speak-er phones, or hands-free phones will be provided
- whether modems or fax modems will be necessary
- whether fax machines will be provided (what capabilities)
- whether copy machines will be provided
- how supplies will be handled
- how maintenance and repair will be handled.

Some of the policies and procedures are not quite as obvious but are very normal, for example:

- Who will move these and other items from the office to the home office, if necessary?
- Who will set up the technology in the home office or load the software, or do both?
- How many phone lines will be necessary, what type, and are they for the company's use only?

- Can laptop computers be substituted for desktops if new computers need to be purchased?
- How will phone messages be handled at the home office and at the company office (voice mail, machine, roll over)?
- How will emergency needs for supplies be dealt with?
- How will requests for specialized equipment be handled?

Some policies and procedures are neither obvious nor normal, but can be very important under certain circumstances. Following are several examples:

- When is an accident with the machinery negligence, and what happens then? For example, if the telecommuter's child sits on the keyboard or an in-law drops the monitor, is the telecommuter negligent? (These are both real-life examples in which a company felt the telecommuter was negligent.)
- Can the employee use his or her own personal machines in lieu of company provided ones, and how does that affect maintenance and repair? (If a company lets its telecommuter use his or her own answering machine and it breaks, who buys a new one, and who owns it if the telecommuter leaves the company?)
- When and how can telecommuters use company equipment for private processes? Can the employee keep his or her own records on a company computer? How about the spouse's recipes? The daughter's term paper? Is there a foreseeable end to these types of questions?
- What type of security for equipment and data is expected? How will passwords be assigned and used? What kind of doors and locks will be required? Although the latter question might more properly belong in the work space area, I have included it here because it has a strong security aspect. I encountered one company that required locks on all home offices, and another that required deadbolts on all outside doors of the home. Both paid for this process (thankfully), but both received complaints from homemakers that the workers were messy. I didn't have the heart to ask if the locks were to be removed if the employees

left the company. Another question is, who arranges for these processes and how soon must they be completed.

- How do you control Internet use? The policy ramifications of Internet access are bad enough in the office environment, but in the home office environment, they are mind boggling. How do you know when it's being used? Who polices it? When is Big Brother just too much? Even with fire walls, how does a company stop telecommuters from using the company's phone line for their own computer? I have no answers, just a one-word comment: Trust.

### SUPPORT

The last group of policies and procedures in the technology category relate to support for the telecommuter. It is much more difficult for MIS people to support 50 telecommuters working an average of 30 miles from the main office than it is to support the same 50 people down the hall or even in a neighboring building. If a machine goes down, new software needs to be loaded, or a hardware upgrade added, MIS faces a much more time- and labor-intensive process to support telecommuters than in-office staff.

The company's policies and procedures need to cover aspects such as the optimum (and possibly maximum) amount of time to effect repairs and how the increased costs will be handled. The telecommuting committee should have taken these contingencies into account during the telecommuting cost-benefit analysis, and it should have consulted with the technology department on these issues. It is now necessary to get that department's suggestions on how the policies and procedures should be written.

Other policies and procedures issues in the same general area include the establishment of a help desk for telecommuters who have technology problems or questions and a plan for loaner or rental machines if the telecommuter's machine needs to be taken out of service for an untenable period. Remember that one of the major disadvantages of telecommuting is the reduced availability of backup if things break. This problem must be taken into account in the policies and procedures.

Another support aspect for inclusion in the procedures is the telecommuting ombudsman. Whether one or more people hold the job, the ombudsman is often responsible for helping employees begin telecommuting, troubleshooting nontechnical problems, and interpreting telecommuting policies and procedures. As such, the ombudsman needs to know what his or her responsibilities are and how to go about the job. A policy that recognizes the importance of this position helps, as do procedures that set out plans and limitations. The policy and procedure should describe how to get in touch with the ombudsman.

Another function of this position might be to monitor and evaluate the system. We discussed the policies and procedures for this aspect earlier, with one of the questions being who does it. Now you have a who whose personal job procedures you can dovetail into the monitoring and evaluation ones.

## Human Resources

The third category of policies and procedures deals with human resources processes. Once again, there will be some overlap. It is also important to reiterate that the legal staff should review these policies and procedures.

### COMPENSATION

In general, compensation for telecommuters should be determined in the same way as that of their nontelecommuting counterparts. This arrangement should be stated as policy as should any changes to this rule that are necessary in a company's business environment.

### STARTING AND STOPPING TIMES

The workday is is a critical issue. As noted in chapter 2, one of the advantages of telecommuting is that telecommuters can work when they are most effective. Unfortunately, this policy creates problems in some organizations. HR telecommuting policies need to state explicitly the time availabilities that companies expect of telecommuters. The most effective approach is to specify the expected number of hours per day, and no further stipulations. The least effective approach is to say "regular business hours." However, the best approach for each company is what works best for it.

Whenever possible, companies should allow supervisors some latitude. Companies may need to have a stringent policy, but it is best to allow some supervisor discretionary flexibility. Although that policy presents another training issue for supervisors, the benefit will far outweigh this minor disadvantage.

### RECORD KEEPING

It would be expensive to place a time clock in every telecommuter's home, and even the most liberal of employers will admit that telecommuting opens the door for work time abuse. Some companies have instituted a computer-based time and attendance system in which telecommuters sign in and out on their computer. Of course, signing in doesn't necessarily mean working.

There are also monitoring programs that can allow supervisors to see in either real time or on a computer-generated record how much work is being done, up to and including the number of key strokes per hour. However, companies that are that worried about these matters are probably not suited to telecommuting.

Successful telecommuting is based on trust. Companies need policies and procedures to help define the process, and even to monitor it, but not to overcontrol it. If the trust isn't there, the chances of a successful telecommuting intervention become very small indeed.

In the final analysis, record-keeping procedures are simply to keep track of hours for compensation. They should be as simple as possible for that particular HR purpose. Supervisors who want to look at how hard their telecommuters are working should monitor productivity measures or keep the employees in the office and place a supervisor over their shoulder at all times.

## OFFICE DAYS

A related HR issue is the policy concerning days in the office. The telecommuter should always have office days planned in accordance with what the company believes is the right number of days in a week, month, or year for them to make a physical appearance. Opinions differ on what this is, and I've seen systems ranging from three days per week to once in a blue moon.

It's not good for the telecommuter to be gone too long from the office, or the employee may face the disadvantages that come from being out of sight. A good rule of thumb is to have an office day at least once a week or to keep the telecommuter at least partially plugged in, at the minimum of once a month.

A company should base its policy on what is best for it and its telecommuters. Once again, supervisor discretion is not a bad approach if the supervisors are trained to use that discretion wisely.

A company may choose to develop procedures concerning what the telecommuter should do during office days, though I think beyond some general guidelines that is best left to the supervisor and the telecommuter.

## EMPLOYEE BENEFITS

Generally employee benefits for telecommuters should follow the same policy as those for compensation; they should be no different than those for other comparable employees who don't telecommute. However, experiences have shown the following effects on some benefits:

- **Sick time:** There is a decrease in sick time among telecommuters, particularly in mental health days. It is a good idea to establish a procedure for telecommuters to report that they are taking a sick day. Usually they directly notify their supervisor.

- **Holiday pay:** Companies may need to establish procedures on how to report if telecommuters decide to work during a holiday. Being at home to begin with makes this an attractive situation at times. The policy should describe time or money compensation (you may have to write one if you don't already have one or you may need to modify an existing one).
- **Overtime:** This is one of the stickiest policy and procedures questions for telecommuting. If all of the telecommuters are salaried, the problem is more one of fairness than record keeping. For hourly telecommuters, record keeping is the paramount issue. My experience is that those who are involved in telecommuting situations should do what is right and be certain that the written procedures reflect that.
- **Personal days:** Telecommuters and nontelecommuters should get equal treatment. However, some companies institute a partial personal day policy for telecommuters, allowing them to use half days and even personal hours at their supervisors' discretion. The companies' rationale is that these workers are geographically close to both the locations for their personal activities and work. You can see the record-keeping problem here if you get too strict, but there is also a fairness issue for nontelecommuters that needs to be considered.

## WORKERS' COMPENSATION AND OTHER INSURANCE

Simply stated, the employee is an employee whether working at home, in the office, or on the road. Therefore telecommuters should be considered covered while at work at home, just as any other employee is in the office. This policy can get a bit questionable if the telecommuter's hours are not standard, but a company's policy should state that work is work, no matter what the environment.

Policies and procedures should state specifically what types of insurance coverage the employee has through the company and what types telecommuters are expected to have for themselves, others (liability is a major issue), and their dwelling. Policies should clarify who is responsible if there is no insurance, or if the insurance company does not pay.

## TRAVEL

Although it should be understood, it is usually worthwhile to state that the organization's travel policy does not cover travel to the office on office days. It is also good to have a policy concerning any travel reimbursement as it relates to the telecommuter's home as the business place.

## TERMINATION

There are two aspects to termination. One is terminating of the telecommuting process, and the other is the actual termination of a telecommuter.

It is as important to state how a telecommuter and his or her supervisor would terminate the telecommuting process and effect a return to the office as it is to state how they start the initiative. Remember, not everyone is cut out to be a telecommuter, and even the best assessment processes will make mistakes. A company's policy needs to lay out the specific situations and reasons that will be considered acceptable for termination of telecommuting and any negative aspects that might be involved. Some organizations use a review committee or at least a meeting with the telecommuting ombudsman to certify termination. Others have a form for this purpose. Who makes the final decision is a key issue here.

Procedures need to detail timelines and contacts for dismantling of the home office and for reassembling of the business office. A checklist for the soon-to-be former telecommuter, the supervisor, and other involved parties is a useful tool.

Terminating employment of a telecommuter has its own problems and needs specific procedures to deal with them. The most important concern is the return of company equipment and records.

Each company handles these processes differently, but every company should address these issues. It is not likely that a company's current procedures for in-office termination will provide enough detail to be effective in a telecommuting environment.

Another concern has to do with fairness. The words of one supervisor I talked to are probably more telling than anything I might say. "I've got to let someone go. How can I lay off a person who comes to work every day before I lay off a telecommuter?" You need a termination policy that clearly indicates that telecommuters are just as much workers as anyone else.

## UNION CONTRACTS

Unionized companies should have union representatives help draft their telecommuting policies and their HR policies. As in everything else that has to do with changes in employment, the unions should be a partner in any initiative that is good for their members and the organization. They should be involved early and remain part of the process.

## OTHER CHANGES TO STANDARD WORK RULES

Other standard work rules may need revision because of telecommuting. It is a good idea to make these revisions organization-wide, not just for the telecommuters. A sure way to build animosity between the telecommuters and their colleagues who do not telecommute is to make it appear that the telecommuters are being given special privileges. Nontelecommuters who believe they are being unfairly treated can easily sabotage the system, either directly or indirectly by simply not helping to support the telecommuters who need them if they are to function effectively.

When it is necessary to have different policies, it is important to explain very clearly why this is so to the nontelecommuters during their training sessions and to ask for suggestions to reduce the disparity. Also, discussions with the nontelecommuters should be a major part of monitoring. During these discussions, it is essential to ask them how the policy changes are affecting them.

## Tax Liability

Almost nobody wants to talk about tax liability. The tax codes on home offices are so complicated that even good accountants suggest not to bother with them. A company's policy should state that the telecommuter is an employee and not a contractor. He or she falls under all the tax advantages and liabilities of an employee. Therefore, the employee is responsible for any tax liability he or she incurs in defining the situation in any other way.

Of course, companies that decide to pay rent to the employee for use of his or her house or that reimburse the employee for utility bills, equipment, or repairs have created a whole new set of circumstances and need a new set of policies and procedures to deal with them. This brings up the fourth category of procedures, financial.

## Financial

So far in this chapter, the discussion has touched on some candidates for these policies and procedures. Following is a list of some financial policies and procedures:

- **Equipment:** Who will pay for basic equipment? What reimbursement policies are in effect? Will any rent be paid on employee equipment? Who will decide on and buy replacement equipment?
- **Phones:** Who will pay for phone installation, monthly bills, repair, and even the phones themselves? How will this be done? If necessary, how will personal and office portions be calculated?
- **Furniture:** Will the company pay for or provide basic furniture (desks, files, tables, stands, and the like)? If employee furniture will be used, will a rental charge be paid? Who pays for repair, replacement, or wear and tear?
- **Special furniture and equipment:** If special furniture or equipment (scanners, hands-free phones, postage machines, and so forth) are needed, who will pay and how should these things be approved and ordered?

- **Physical plant:** If remodeling needs to be done to make the home environment acceptable or because of changes to the telecommuter's job, who will pay, and who will approve? Will the company pay rent for the work space?
- **Utilities:** Will the company pay a percentage of the utilities, and if so how will this be calculated?
- **Insurance:** Will the company pay for a portion of the present insurance or for special insurance for liability, home, or contents if required?
- **Maintenance and repair:** Who will pay for maintenance and repair of business-related machines, both normally and in emergency situations? Who will authorize emergencies?
- **Loaner machines:** Who will cover the cost of loaner machines when and if necessary?
- **Couriers:** Who will pay for overnight deliveries and other forms of special delivery back to the office, and who will authorize them?
- **Handicapped employees:** Who pays for any construction or equipment needed to meet the needs of employees with disabilities? This policy has major ADA implications and should be carefully stated.

One of the more general questions a company needs to ask is what cost centers will provide it with the funds? Will things be charged to a special telecommuting account? If so, who authorizes expenditures and is responsible for the account? Will the telecommuter's department pay for all or part of the expenses? How will this be budgeted?

In most organizations, expenditures are treated the same as if the telecommuter was on-site. Thus the responsible department or system picks up the technology expenses, supplies are a department responsibility, refurbishment comes from capital accounts, and so forth. This arrangement makes it easy to write the procedures but difficult to track expenses that may be a major part of a telecommuting evaluation. No matter how a company decides to do it, it should be sure that an inability to get expense authorizations does not hamstring telecommuters and, therefore, a program.

The financial policies and procedures, along with other policies and procedures, may seem to have gotten a bit out of hand. However, this chapter has presented all the possibilities, not just the most common ones. There are many financial advantages for the telecommuter, commuting expenses being the largest of them. Most telecommuting systems work under the premise that the financial disadvantages and advantages balance each other, and almost all telecommuters would agree. Few would not be willing to pay for a little more electricity if it meant their car would sit home three days a week or so.

What is important is that a company's policies and procedures be complete enough so that there would be no surprises, or at least as few as humanly possible for everyone involved. The policies and procedures will also guide a company's training, implementation, and evaluation. So even though preparing them may seem to be a heavy task, it is worth spending the time to do them right.

## Summary of Telecommuting Policies and Procedures

Following is a checklist of the elements that are important to include in telecommuting policies and procedures:
- [ ] Telecommuting eligibility
  - Selection criteria
  - Telecommuting application
- [ ] Telecommuting contract
- [ ] Telecommuting committee
- [ ] Training
- [ ] Monitoring
- [ ] Evaluation
- [ ] Moving out/moving in
- [ ] Work space

☐ Hardware and supplies
☐ Support
☐ Human resources
  • Compensation
  • Benefits
  • Changes to standard work rules
  • Workers' compensation and insurance
  • Travel
  • Termination
  • Tax liability
  • Financial

# 5

# Introducing the Organization to Telecommuting

---

*"Have good reasons, and talk them over in detail with your supervisor....Oh, and the rest of your group too."*
— Experienced Telecommuter

---

The saying that well begun is half done may not be true all the time, but it may be an understatement for readers who have done the preliminary tasks described to this point and have gone on to create an effective plan for introducing their telecommuting intervention. They may be even more than half done.

## Who Needs to Know?

Telecommuting is a major organizational intervention, and everyone in the organization needs to know something about it, though some employees need to know more than others. To cover this large an audience with such diverse needs, companies must have a number of components in their introduction plan. A good way to start is for a member of the telecommuting committee or another advocate to give a presentation about telecommuting to top management.

## Top Management

The assumption in this discussion is that top management does not need to be sold on the idea of telecommuting. Readers who have been taking the suggestions in this book have put a lot of effort and a not insignificant amount of corporate resources into their telecommuting intervention, and that could only have been done with top management's blessing.

Chapter 2 described the reasons an organization might choose to explore telecommuting, but did not discuss an exploration by what might be termed initiators. An initiator could be anyone from the chief executive officer to a department head who wants to undertake an exploration of telecommuting. If there is only one initiator (for example, the reader) or a few (perhaps the reader and his or her boss or a few other people with vision), then the job ahead is much bigger because they will have to sell top management on both telecommuting and their plan. This discussion will provide some help to the initiators, but they will need to present a lot more detail and a much more intensive sales presentation than this book covers. The process in this chapter is for communicating a telecommuting plan after corporate decision makers have agreed to the concept.

When top management is more or less sold on the idea of telecommuting, the telecommuting committee or responsible individual who is introducing the organization to telecommuting is presenting a review of what it has already done and learned. The primary emphasis should be on the reasons the committee is recommending a telecommuting intervention (from chapter 2), the vision and philosophy the committee worked out (from chapter 3), and the policies and procedures it proposes (from chapter 4). The presentation will include detail on the cost estimates (from chapter 3) and any particular changes to existing policies and procedures, which may be a problem in the particular corporate culture. In most initiatives, it will be necessary to get a good deal of backing from this level of the organization to make these policy and procedure changes.

The presentation should conclude with a review of the advantages of telecommuting and possibly a little envisioning of the company in the future, complete with satisfied productive employees in a telecommuting environment, better bottom lines, and a corporate award for community service for reducing pollution. Even if top management is already sold, it doesn't hurt to remind the members of what they are buying. This vision can be brought up again later when problems occur, which they will, and the advocates need the managers' help.

The introduction to top management is to prepare them to lend their **active** support to the intervention. It is to inspire them so that they'll give their support by writing memos, holding meetings, and possibly even taking part in the training and monitoring processes. It is to get them to present the initiative favorably to their staff and to others in the organization with whom they interact. A hoped-for outcome of the introduction is that top-level managers would allow their staff to attend the telecommuting orientation meetings and perhaps go further by strongly recommending that they go. The managers should also leave the meeting with the understanding that there will be some problems and rough spots, but the presenters' intention is that the managers will coach their people to keep with it and will provide the leadership that will help make telecommuting work. Another outcome may be that top-level managers will find themselves on videotape explaining the importance of telecommuting to more than just their direct subordinates.

In some telecommuting interventions, the top managers have been asked to sign their own form of a telecommuting agreement, detailing their responsibilities in the plan. In others, the CEOs have challenged them to choose from a list of things that needed to be done, such as presenting written policies or holding a meeting with their direct reports to introduce telecommuting to them; this gets them involved in the process on a companywide platform. In still others, top managers receive a to-do list with items requiring attention, such as sending a memo to all their employees discussing telecommuting in their own words and meeting with each group of chosen telecommuters from their area to congratulate them and give them a pep talk before they go out.

A top management introduction can be as simple or structured as the corporate culture and telecommuting intervention requires. Whatever the style, it is a good idea to start at the top with a telecommuting introduction.

It is important to note that if, after the introduction, presenters can't get the commitment to active support the intervention needs, it is time to reconsider telecommuting for the organization. Effective telecommuting is an organization-wide intervention, and not a particularly easy road to travel. There will be problems, people who refuse to accept the plan, supervisors and even telecommuters who can't deal with the changes. When these difficulties occur, the people responsible for the program will need support for some tough decisions. Lack of support in the early stages is almost a guarantee that support won't be there later, and that will lead to the initiative's failure.

## Introducing Others

The next introductions to telecommuting vary with the size of the organization. In large companies, it may be necessary to introduce telecommuting to several layers of management to garner more support. This is an important step in a large company environment. As many corporate change agents have found to their dismay, simply having top management support doesn't mean the lower levels automatically give their support.

It is important to know who the real implementers are in an organization and to tailor an introduction especially for them. The presenters should explain how the intervention will benefit them directly, their people, and the company as well, probably in that order. They should give the implementers something to do to help enact the program or somehow be a part of it and develop a sense of ownership for it. This activity may be as simple as holding a next level meeting, volunteering one of their groups for a pilot study, or volunteering themselves to serve on the telecommuting committee or in a monitoring role. It also won't hurt to have supportive top managers at these introductions to lend some authority and possibly even help with the presentation.

## The Telecommuting Orientation

After the people at the upper and middle levels understand telecommuting, it will be necessary to run a general telecommuting orientation. The telecommuting orientation should be open to all interested employees regardless of what the plan is. These orientations are mandatory in some organizations.

The logic of inviting employees to an orientation if they are not going to be part of the process is threefold. First, it is to stop the grapevine from buzzing with rumors about telecommuting, and second it is to gain buy-in. Employee acceptance is important even among those who won't be participating because they may still be supporting the telecommuters.

A third reason is that trust is developed by letting people in on what is going on. Companies that are guided by this philosophy should have no trouble getting people to their orientation. Companies that are not may need to ask for some upper-level support to give everyone a chance to see what telecommuting is all about.

### Memos

The first step in the orientation is for the top people at each level to send memos endorsing telecommuting to staff at the next level. The new senders may attach copies of the upper-level memos to their memos. If this procedure seems too complicated for your situation, a memo from the CEO will do fine.

These memos should explain why the organization is promoting telecommuting; include some specific advantages for employees, the organization, and the community; and end with a recommendation that everyone attend the orientation to find out more. Some companies may require a more formal approach, and perhaps a requirement instead of a recommendation. In any case, the memos should be short and simple. Their purpose is to show support from higher levels and to get people to the orientation.

## Media

The orientation does not need to be long, and depending on a company's level of technical capability, it doesn't even have to be live. Companies have used audiotapes, videotapes, CD-ROMs, computer networks, and even satellite networks to provide a telecommuting orientation.

Whatever the medium, the orientation should cover a few key issues:

- the organization's definition of telecommuting
- the organization's telecommuting vision
- the advantages and disadvantages of telecommuting, with particular attention paid to those that were most important in the decision to implement a telecommuting program and to the advantages and disadvantages to employees
- eligibility requirements
- what the next step in the process is and when it is expected.

It is imperative to address all the expectations fully and completely. Particularly when all staff have been invited to the orientation, the presenters need to keep the expectations of the audience clear about who in the audience can expect to be considered for telecommuting. About the worst thing a company could do to the program and the employees at this point is to delay decision about eligibility or waffle on it.

Following the formal presentation, there should be plenty of time available for questions. Presenters should be ready for some controversy, particularly concerning eligibility. If the committee did a complete job of analyzing and planning the program, it should be able to handle these questions logically and honestly.

Companies that use technology-based orientations will need to develop some method for answering questions. One successful approach is the hot-line phone number staffed by people who know the answers or can find them quickly. The least effective method is to give direct supervisors the available information about telecommuting and have them answer the questions. There are two fallacies with this method. The first is that it is possible to predict all the answers to all the possible questions and provide them. The second is that the supervisors will understand and be able to explain properly all the answers. Telecommuting is a new concept for many employees, and particularly for supervisors it is one that is fraught with personal questions. At best, it is a suspect approach to ask supervisors to assume even more responsibility in explaining and answering questions about a process that they are likely to be wary of. People who understand how telecommuting will work in the organization and can deal with the tough questions in a manner consistent with the organization's needs are the best choice for answering questions.

This is not to say the supervisors can't help. A helpful approach is to create a supervisors' orientation to give them added depth into telecommuting. The committee or anyone else responsible may send them a packet of information on telecommuting and may even begin a supervisors' telecommuting newsletter, though this is more in the aspect of continuing publicity which is discussed later. These types of endeavors can go a long way toward making supervisors proponents of the initiative.

Technologically oriented organizations or those with technology-based communications processes can use their intranet or corporate electronic bulletin board to answer telecommuting questions. These methods would even work well in companies that do a live orientation because questions may come up after the orientation is over when employees have had time to digest the information.

Companies can also distribute a list of possible questions and their answers. This method can reduce the number of questions at technologically based programs and reinforce discussions at live orientations. As the initiative continues, the committee can add new questions and their answers to this list from earlier orientation groups.

In one audiotape introduction to telecommuting that I worked on, questions and answers were part of a simulated supervisory discussion on telecommuting. Five voices represented a narrator, a supervisor, and three employees. The employees on the tape asked questions that the target audience might have, and the supervisor and narrator provided the basic introduction to telecommuting.

An introduction like this could also work well on videotape or even in a computer-generated environment. Like any technology, however, a presentation technology that would be expensive or difficult to modify is not a good idea if there could be changes in the simulation.

Top management was helpful with the memo and can also be helpful in furthering the initiative's credibility by presenting an orientation message. Although a live message is best, a videotaped message will suffice. In fact, if a live message has been planned, a videotape backup is almost mandatory because no matter how good a manager's intentions, top management priorities may win out over the orientation.

## Special Telecommuting Introductions

In addition to the general orientation, some other meetings introducing telecommuting may be advisable. These could include the targeted audience for telecommuting, their supervisors, and possibly their supervisors (that is, the department managers). Because each of these audiences will need more information about their role in the telecommuting process than the general orientation would provide, it is a good idea to hold special introductions for them. These meetings could take place in mixed groups or with each group separately, depending on whether the employees and their supervisors are comfortable in meetings with multiple levels in attendance.

Companies that address each level separately should try to hold the meetings simultaneously, or as close to that as possible. It tends to send the wrong message if all department heads are covered first, then the supervisors, and last, and what may seem like least, the proto-telecommuters.

## Continued Publicity

After the orientation, and continuing for probably as long as telecommuting, it is necessary to publicize the program. Publicity is particularly critical in the beginning, as the intervention gains momentum and acceptance. The need may diminish somewhat as the system matures, but publicity should never be entirely neglected.

Newsletters, bulletin boards (both electronic and the old-fashioned kind), memos, and live updates are the normal publicity techniques. Another possibility is to place articles in the corporate news organ, perhaps even a continuing column. These communications are to tout the program, answer questions, and squelch rumors before they get too far along.

A supervisors' newsletter is effective in responding to supervisory questions and problems that arise, and it can also function for continued training. The newsletter works best if the telecommuters' supervisors write articles themselves or at least are interviewed for stories.

Management and top-management newsletters may also be useful for ongoing publicity in companies that have the resources for them. Otherwise they do not justify the expenditure of time. A more efficient approach is to send the supervisors' newsletter or even the general newsletter to higher management, perhaps with a half-page cover note drawing their attention to any particular items.

A less formal approach is to place in the cafeteria or any other employee areas a three-fold company brochure about telecommuting. Some companies even hand out reprints of new magazine articles about telecommuting in this way or circulate them by company mail.

Companies with intranet can do all of these things electronically. One word of warning: With all the e-mail managers complain about getting, that system is not a good one to use for publicizing telecommuting.

## Getting Started

The final item in the organizational introduction to telecommuting is to explain to would-be telecommuters how to get started. The committee should have outlined this process in the policies and procedures. This is the place to flesh out the description so that everyone understands what to do next.

### Department Managers

First, it is necessary to obtain commitments for telecommuting from the managers or department heads. During their orientation meetings, presenters could tell them how to proceed if they are interested. A more formal approach would be to have them, and even their superior if necessary, sign some type of written departmental telecommuting agreement. This document should not be more than a page in length and should lay out the department's responsibilities in the program. Responsibilities can run from simply providing general support to providing specific responsibility for choosing groups and even individuals, and supplying equipment. This document does not take the place of the telecommuting contract, but simply augments it.

The importance of departmental buy-in is so great that in most initiatives if the department head doesn't commit, the process should go no further in that department. It is possible that some employees in a particular group would like to telecommute, but if the department head was not swayed by the orientations and publicity, the employees must be excluded from the program. They would most likely fail as telecommuters because of lack of support, and their failure may bring down the whole initiative.

It often happens that after a telecommuting intervention is under way and successful, some of these recalcitrant department heads will have second thoughts. However, except in the most extreme cases of required telecommuting, it is not a good idea to force the issue with them or to have their boss force it.

## Employee Level

After the department heads have signed up, the employee process can begin. Depending on the company, the emphasis turns to the telecommuting application or to explanations of the procedures to interested parties. Companies that use a telecommuting application may want to hold follow-up sessions with possible candidates to discuss how to complete it, particularly if it is detailed in nature. The special telecommuting introductions for target audiences would be a good place to explain the applications.

A telecommuting application, even a very simple one with nothing more than personal information, contact numbers, and a place for a signature, helps to organize the process and keep track of telecommuters. It is a good way to start the process, and I highly recommend it. Examples of simple and complex telecommuting applications appear in the appendix at the end of this chapter.

The criteria that will be used to choose telecommuters should be considered part of the getting-started materials. The committee laid these out in its procedures, but possible candidates need to be able to access them as well.

Some companies use a checklist format, and others use a suitability survey of some type. The next chapter focuses in more detail on telecommuting surveys, but they also may be part of the getting-started process.

The purpose of providing the selection criteria as part of the getting-started process is to do an early winnowing of candidates. It is important to be clear and concise about the criteria and follow them closely so those who won't fit won't waste anyone's time, including their own, in the selection process.

The would-be telecommuters' direct supervisor should become involved in the process as soon as possible, ideally when employees are thinking about signing up. A special supervisors' information session should take place during this early stage so they can learn details of the getting-started process, selection of the telecommuters, and the supervisors' role. In many initiatives, supervisors have the final say in who becomes a telecommuter, or they have at least an important recommendation.

Some telecommuting interventions use a supervisors' contract to augment the telecommuting contract. The information session is a good place to introduce them to the contract.

## Telecommuting Prototype

It is advisable to run a prototype before implementing telecommuting in all departments. The prototype typically has one of two major purposes, publicity or piloting the actual telecommuting mechanism. There are about as many ways to run a prototype as there are telecommuting interventions.

If publicity is the goal, it's a good idea to start with a lot of hoopla and then keep all staff apprised of how well the telecommuters are doing through the normal publicity channels. A small prototype with closely controlled and handpicked telecommuter winners who make sure everything goes as smoothly as possible works well for this purpose.

If the pilot is to look for problems and areas that need improvement, it is best to implement the prototype exactly as it will run when rolled out to the entire organization. Companies that want to pilot for both publicity and troubleshooting together, the most common reason, should also take this approach. The telecommuters would then have to be chosen through the planned procedures, not handpicked, and they would have to receive the support they would normally get, dealing with day-to-day issues as they occur. They and their supervisors could not get more intensive training than everyone else would get, nor could they get assistance to make it easier for them to get their equipment or set up their home offices. The telecommuting committee will only get the right information from the prototype if no one goes around checking on the telecommuters every day and solving problems as they occur.

This approach means that a few telecommuters will fail. The important thing is to let the prototype intervention run pretty much as it would during the full-fledged program. One area that the committee should augment for the prototype is monitoring. If the purpose is to find procedures that need help, or simply rough spots that need a little smoothing, it is important to monitor closely those aspects that might be a problem.

It will be tempting to change things as the monitoring indicates that improvements are needed. Some people may call it tinkering. My advice is don't tinker! The prototype won't give accurate information if changes take place. It is important to watch and record, but not act until the prototype has run its course. It will be difficult to hold off, particularly if the committee is hoping for good publicity but instead finds that a number of telecommuters are having a hard time.

The time to make changes is after the prototype and before the first rollout. If the prototype indicates that major changes are necessary, it may be necessary to run a second prototype to determine the effectiveness of the changes. In that case, changes should not take place until all the data are in. Some problems take care of themselves, and sometimes telecommuters come up with novel approaches to take care of others.

It is important to let the first telecommuters know that they are going out as guinea pigs. They should be made aware that the prototype might not be as easy or smooth as one might hope. The committee should get plenty of feedback from them, and if it is possible, offer the ones who don't make it a chance to try again after the company has fixed the problems. The committee should listen to their ideas and implement the good ones, but be sure the telecommuters understand that these fixes won't occur until the prototype has run its course.

## A Checklist for Introducing Telecommuting

Following is a checklist of the elements that are important to resolve in introducing telecommuting to an organization:

☐ Top management is sold on the concept.
- If not, what are you going to do to change that?

☐ The top management introduction includes:
- Reasons for recommending telecommuting
- Vision
- Philosophy
- Summarized policies and procedures
- Cost estimates
- Review of the advantages
- Request for active support.

☐ Specific introductions for other management layers are ready and include:
- A way to build active ownership in the program.

☐ The general orientation is ready.
- Endorsement memos from higher up have begun making the rounds and include the vision, definition, advantages and disadvantages (for everyone), eligibility requirements, and the next step to take.
- Top management representative will be present to add credibility.
- Program addresses employees' expectations so no one will get the wrong idea.

☐ Special telecommuting introductions are ready for the following:
- Department managers
- Supervisors
- The target audience.

- [ ] Plans for continued publicity are under way.
- [ ] Department managers know how to get started.
  - Departmental telecommuting agreement is ready.
- [ ] Target employees know how to get started.
  - Telecommuting application is ready.
  - Selection criteria are clear.
  - The suitability survey is ready.
- [ ] Supervisors know their getting-started roles.
  - Supervisors' orientation is ready.
  - Supervisors understand the role of their recommendations.
  - Supervisor's telecommuting contract is ready.
- [ ] The prototype plan has been formulated.
  - Its purposes are clear.
  - Monitoring is planned.

# Appendix

# Telecommuting Application, Type 1

Name _____

Supervisor(s) _____

Position _____

Department _____

Extension _____

E-mail address _____

1. Does your job permit you to telecommute, at least part of the time? _____

2. How long have you been in your current job? _____

3. Has your supervisor(s) responded favorably to your becoming a telecommuter? _____

4. Home telephone _____

5. Home address _____

   _____

6. Do you wish to telecommute? ☐ yes ☐ no

7. How many days per week would you like to telecommute?


_____          _____
Employee's Signature                                    Date

I believe this employee should be considered for telecommuting:


_____          _____
Supervisor's Signature                                   Date

# Telecommuting Application, Type 2

Name: _____

Employee #: _____Department: _____

Extension:_____ Location: _____ Mailstop: _____

**Job Responsibilities:**

_____

_____

Length of Employment: _____ Title: _____

Last Performance Appraisal Rating: _____

## Work Characteristics

*Please rate the following according to your existing job requirements and characteristics:*

H for HIGH, M for MEDIUM, L for LOW

_____ Amount of face-to-face contact required

_____ Ability to organize face-to-face communications into predetermined time period

_____ Degree of telephone communications required

_____ Clarity of objectives for a given work effort

_____ Autonomy of operation

_____ Ability to control and schedule work flow

_____ Amount of in-office reference material required

Describe the types of work you propose to do at home:

## Employee Characteristics

*Please rate yourself according to the following characteristics as an employee:*

H for HIGH, M for MEDIUM, L for LOW

_____ Need for supervision and frequent feedback

_____ Quality of organization and planning skills

_____ Importance of on-site co-workers input to work function

_____ Discipline regarding work

_____ Reliability regarding work hours

_____ Computer literacy level

_____ Desire/need to be around people

_____ Desire for scheduling flexibility for any reason

_____ Potential friction at home of telecommuting (e.g., interruptions from child or spouse)

_____ Level of job knowledge

_____ Productivity

_____ Quality of work

## Manager Characteristics

*Based on your perception of your supervisor's attitude toward telecommuting and his or her management style, please rate your supervisor according to the following:*

H for HIGH, M for MEDIUM, L for LOW

_____ Positive attitude toward telecommuting

_____ Trust employee's ability to telecommute

_____ Organization and planning skills

_____ Ability to establish clear objectives

_____ Provide formal feedback regularly

_____ Flexibility

_____ Ability to communicate with employees

_____ Results and project oriented rather than activity or process oriented (manages by results, not by process)

Do you and your supervisor work in the same office? _____

*Home Office:*

Home Telephone: _____

Home Address: _____

Mailing Address: _____

Description of designated work space at home:

List personal equipment and furniture to be used at home:

Have you discussed this arrangement with your spouse/family?

☐ yes ☐ no

List current desktop computer equipment used at the company:

I would like to work from home _____ days per week.

_____     _____
Employee Signature                              Date

"I have considered this employee's application and recommend him/her as a suitable candidate for telecommuting."

_____     _____     _____
Manager (please print)              Signature                      Date

# 6

# Selecting Employees for Telecommuting

---

*"It's not a cure for a bad family life; in fact, it will probably make it worse."*

—Experienced Telecommuter

---

One of the hardest jobs in a telecommuting intervention is selecting the right people to telecommute. Doing it effectively will save an organization money, its employees frustration, and the program from possible disaster.

## Why People Choose to Telecommute

Of all the quotes that introduce the chapters of this book, the one that starts this chapter may be the most telling. Many people regard telecommuting as an answer to their problems at home, whether the problems are financial or personal. Their difficulties may have to do with child care or elder care. They may simply stem from one spouse's complaints that the other is never home to help around the house. Whatever the underlying personal problems that may motivate an employee into considering telecommuting, it is not the cure. Telecommuting is simply a different way to work. It has advantages and disadvantages, some of which are related to an employee's personal time and convenience. However, telecommuting won't cure a bad family life or anything else of that nature. Would-be telecommuters need to understand this from day one.

## Who Chooses?

When the telecommuting committee set down the program's eligibility requirements in its policies and procedures, it made one of its most important decisions concerning telecommuter selection. There are more aspects to telecommuter selection than just eligibility, however. The most basic of these is who makes the decision that an employee will explore the process in detail and possibly become a telecommuter.

In most telecommuting interventions, the interested employee and that person's supervisor together arrive at the decision. Initially, the employee may express an interest either informally to the supervisor or through a more formal procedure, such as the telecommuting application. This step usually takes place after the general telecommuting orientation. The supervisor concurs or not on the basis of the eligibility criteria and his or her own perception of the situation.

However, there are two ways in which employees are chosen: self-nomination by the employees, or with no employee participation. In the first, employees are totally responsible for making the decision to pursue telecommuting. This practice usually occurs in companies in which the motivation for telecommuting is very strong, and after a lot of planning has been done with department and supervisory-level staff to pave the way for employees to be supported if they make this decision. In most cases, self-nomination is only the start of the selection process, and not everyone who decides to do so will become a telecommuter. Everyone who wants to look into telecommuting, however, is given the opportunity.

Self-nomination also takes place in corporate environments that have a self-managed process such as a participative management-based organization. Self-directed work team environments also often allow employees to self-nominate, normally with the team's advice, but not necessarily its permission.

Self-nomination is the norm in some companies, and the programs have been extraordinarily successful, with high productivity and low turnover. These companies are alike in that they have been practicing participative management processes for years, and it is not unusual for them to use self-nomination for many corporate processes. Unless a company has long experience in letting employees make their own decisions, I would not use this approach to nominating individuals for telecommuting. Employees who haven't had long experience in looking at problems and possibilities as part of self-directed teams are not accustomed to undertaking the thoroughgoing analysis that would include the company's perspective.

Companies that give employees no part in the decision-making process have an involuntary or mandatory telecommuting environment. Such interventions are very unusual but do occur, particularly in organizations that are experiencing a crisis and have determined that telecommuting may help solve some of their problems. This approach is not advisable. Telecommuting is difficult enough to implement in a smooth-running organization, so it should be considered most carefully before being attempted in a troubled company. However, a few companies have implemented telecommuting to reduce costs and increase employee productivity when they were in trouble and have found it to be effective.

A more common form of involuntary telecommuting occurs when entire departments are required to telecommute. A company that has to hire additional staff and can't buy or rent more space, for example, may require that employees in one department telecommute. Basically this is one of those if you want to work in this job you are going to telecommute processes. This type of selection process or telecommuting intervention is not advisable because some people are just not suited to be telecommuters, and forcing them into a telecommuting environment almost certainly dooms them to failure.

Somewhat more common is mandatory telecommuting for specific individuals for the good of the organization. This approach usually occurs when the company needs employees to telecommute to make the intervention efficient and produce the advantages it was designed to realize. The obligation is usually put on employees when not enough employees who have been targeted for telecommuting have volunteered to make the process effective. Often this type of selection is coercive. Supervisors who are receiving directives from top management to increase the number of telecommuters may cajole, persuade, and even force employees to sign up for telecommuting. If companies need to do this, it's likely that the telecommuting committee either did a poor job of selling the process or started with the wrong intervention.

These involuntary forms of telecommuting are far and away the exception to the rule, but sometimes they are effective. They require a much more detailed selection and training process than this chapter will cover, but the foundation is the same for voluntary and involuntary selection. However, readers who find themselves saddled with mandatory telecommuting should base their nominations and selections not so much on job categories and hours as on the psychological and home environmental factors of each employee. They may not select the perfect telecommuters this way, but the people they choose will be more satisfied with their lot than those who would have been chosen simply by job classification.

## The Selection Process

Whether the telecommuting intervention is voluntary or mandatory, self-nominated or consensus driven, it will require a process for choosing employees who will have the best chance of being successful at telecommuting and for beginning their transition from office workers to telecommuters. This process should provide all responsible parties with the information they need to decide if it is logical for an individual to pursue telecommuting to the next level.

A number of methods are available, and depending on a company's resources, organizational environment, and time constraints, it may choose one or any combination of them. Companies will expend a lot of corporate resources on these individuals to make them telecommuters, and the success of the selection program will be determined by their success as telecommuters, so it is important to choose the selection methods well.

## Selection Workshop

Workshops are the most common selection methods. These meetings are basically a continuation of the orientation session, but they cover certain aspects of telecommuting in more detail. Among the issues a selection workshop might explore are the following:

- personal advantages and disadvantages of telecommuting
- the candidate's psychological suitability for telecommuting
- general indicators of telecommuting success
- analysis of personal telecommuting work space
- home life and environment
- the candidate's work and supervisory environment.

An important point to remember is that a selection workshop is not meant to be a training session, although it has some aspects of training. The workshop is actually an intermediate step between the telecommuting orientation and the telecommuter training program. It should not go into detail about items that will be covered in training, nor should it give unneeded information to employees who will not go further in the selection process. It should simply provide enough information so employees can make a selection decision.

The workshop might use selection methods like surveys, instruments, checklists, and even simulations along with discussions. These methods are also effective if companies choose to select telecommuters on an individualized basis, rather than through a workshop process. Most of the methods can be used in a technology-based delivery system as well. Some companies that use a combination of methods and techniques have employees complete surveys and other instruments before the workshop. The participants bring the tools with them for discussion. I've found this to be a most effective and efficient method because some employees will decide against telecommuting because of the instruments and checklists.

## Preference Pair Instruments

The selection methods used most often are those that can determine potential candidates' psychological suitability for telecommuting. Typically these are formal questionnaires that present two items at a time and ask for the preference, like the Myers-Briggs Type Indicator questionnaire, though I find it a bit unwieldy for telecommuting purposes. These tools, known as preference pair instruments, range from relatively well-documented forms that are fairly expensive to one- and two-page sheets that cost a few dollars and can be self-scored and analyzed. A reading of the test determines a person's preference type. Many HR departments use preference pair instruments in supervisory training programs or possibly for hiring purposes and can recommend a suitable one.

The key to these formal instruments is to recognize that no preference type is perfectly suited to telecommuting. It might seem obvious from a telecommuting point of view that a preference for introversion would be more suitable than for extroversion, but it is not. Introverts who get too wrapped up in telecommuting, for example, would lose touch with the organization and at times reality. Extroverts could be great telecommuters if their need for interaction was fulfilled on office days or through other processes at home.

It is similarly not obvious whether the judging type or perceiving type would be better telecommuters. Judging types have a psychological strength in that they are normally comfortable with detailed planning. When they are removed from their office, however, they often do not have access to all the resources they feel they need to make decisions. The perceiving types normally have a more difficult time seeing projects through to completion, which is a key attribute of telecommuters, but they adapt well to change, which is what telecommuting is all about.

In general, these instruments are considered helpful tools in selecting telecommuters who are balanced individuals—not overly extroverted or overly introverted, not too sensing or too intuitive. Even this generalization isn't absolute. People who prefer one aspect of a pair strongly over another may still be highly successful telecommuters if they understand how their preferences will affect their telecommuting life and how they can deal with them.

But dealing with preference types who are not suited for telecommuting is work for the training program. The purpose of using these instruments in selection is to help candidates see the opportunities and problems of their psychological preferences, so that they and their supervisor or anyone else responsible can make the best decision concerning their telecommuting suitability.

## Homemade Surveys

Homemade telecommuting surveys are not really scientific enough to warrant the title instrument. Although they may look a lot like a formal instrument, they are seldom validated and they cannot be generalized outside a specific company's environment. They are simply tools that organizations develop that reflect their conceptualizations of telecommuting and what behaviors candidates might exhibit that predict success in the telecommuting initiative. This approach is particularly effective as part of the getting started endeavors, described in chapter 5.

Homemade surveys are easy to use, can be self-scoring, and if well developed are very effective. They deal with any issues that are important to a company's telecommuting environment as well as some psychological suitability items. They can be just about any style an organization requires—long or short, self-scored or other scored, computerized or paper and pencil. They can be free-form, or companies can categorize them into environmental, psychological, family, office, positional, or a whole raft of other factors. Companies can assign different points to more important questions, use a Likert scale, or simply have yes and no answers. Answer sheets can even give the right answers as well as explanations, making them learning tools as well as selection processes.

Like formal instruments, homemade surveys can be tools in a workshop environment or individual selection process or prework for a workshop. However they are put to use, it is important that the people using them understand what they show and their limitations. Some questions from a number of these surveys appear in appendix A at the end of the chapter.

## Simulation

Another method that is useful in the selection process is a telecommuting simulation in which candidates put themselves into the daily life of a telecommuter. In workshop settings, simulations may be as simple as asking candidates to explain free-form how they would work as telecommuters or to respond to questions about their life as telecommuters. More complex written simulations for workshops and individual selection could be fill-in-the-blank processes. A third possibility is to give candidates, either on paper or orally, telecommuting situations and ask how they would handle them.

One of my favorite simulations for a workshop exercise is a variation of the parlor game MadLib that is instructional and fun. It is a fill-in-the-blank exercise that asks employees to provide missing words in a scenario. Unlike the original game, which requested words that fit parts of speech, such as verbs, nouns, adjectives, and adverbs, this exercise often asks for a more specific word, such as time of day or article of clothing. These are placed in a scenario about how a telecommuter spends the day, often with hilarious results. Although the workshop leader will have to redo the scenario later, discussing what would have been logical replies, this combination of humor and repetition seems to help candidates understand

and remember the process of being a telecommuter as they try to make a final selection decision. It also gives the leader some insight into how employees see telecommuting. An excerpt from one of these simulations is in appendix B at the end of the chapter.

A more complex simulation is a computer-mediated approach in which a number of candidates are connected through the company LAN and a conference-call telephone net. For the simulations, candidates develop files and activities, such as sharing information over the LAN, working telephonically in teams to come to a decision on a specific business issue, and sending both e-mail and voice mail. A facilitator moderates the process, but the candidates do most of the talking and all of the work.

The aim is to simulate how a telecommuter works every day. It can be most effective, particularly for those who had never used the technologies before. In my experience with this type of simulation, the group had an online expert who could help those with technology problems get back on track. The process allowed candidates to experience both technology and isolation issues and to get a good feeling for what it might be like if they became telecommuters.

## Checklist Method

One of the most effective selection methods is the simple checklist. Checklists can be used for self-assessment or as a tool for supervisors or others who are responsible for determining telecommuting suitability. Checklists to determine suitable telecommuters may focus on attributes like the following:

- personal traits of successful telecommuters for comparison with candidates'
- work space environment issues to determine if home office plans are conducive to telecommuting
- personal advantages and disadvantages for telecommuting
- home life issues to indicate whether candidates' situations might be supportive of telecommuting.

Checklists can also be used in a workshop, preworkshop, or individualized approach. It is not efficient to have candidates complete checklists during workshops, but companies have had success with asking candidates to complete the checklists before selection workshops and then discuss them at the workshops. Some example checklists are located in appendix C at the end of this chapter.

## Job Analysis

A personal job analysis is a special kind of checklist. During the development of the telecommuting plan, the committee decided which jobs would be the most likely for telecommuting, and possibly even prioritized them. This was a general analysis of job classifications. The purpose of a personal job analysis checklist is to bring this process to the level of the individual employee by allowing each telecommuting candidate to analyze his or her own job. This type of checklist considers not just what the telecommuting candidates do but how they do it and who else might be involved in helping them to do it. It's an analysis of their personal job situation, toward deciding if it will be supportive of telecommuting.

This type of checklist is so individualized that it is not a good workshop tool because its value is in the specificity it provides for each candidate's work environment. The best use for this type of tool is to introduce it in a workshop setting, but have the completion and analysis done on an individual basis. It is often a good mechanism in discussions that candidates and their supervisors have.

## Supervisors and Telecommuter Selection

It is a good idea to have a supervisor's recommendation play a large part in the telecommuter selection process because next to the actual telecommuter, the supervisor is the most important person in the success of the intervention. It is not just a good idea, but almost mandatory that supervisors be involved in the process early and as much as possible.

In an individualized approach to determining telecommuter candidate suitability, the supervisor may even play a critical role in the individual analysis. In some companies, candidates and supervisors attend the selection workshops together and work as a team on surveys, instruments, and checklists.

An unusual but certainly not unheard of tool for the selection process is a supervisor telecommuting suitability survey. This type of survey can be self-analyzed or analyzed with the telecommuter candidate or possibly with the supervisor's manager. Developed and used correctly, it will provide information about whether the supervisor will be supportive of telecommuting, and it can be the beginning of the supervisor's training for telecommuting. Some questions for this type of instrument include the following:

- Does the supervisor have a positive attitude toward telecommuting?
- Do the supervisor and employee exhibit trust in each other?
- Does the supervisor exhibit good planning and time management skills?
- Can the supervisor establish and communicate clear objectives?
- Does the supervisor provide useful regular feedback to the employee?
- Is the supervisor flexible?
- Does the supervisor communicate clearly and regularly with the employee?
- Does the supervisor manage by results and not by time spent at work?
- Does the supervisor do a good job of developing employees?
- Is the supervisor more than just competent at the employee appraisal process?

## Putting It All Together

The data from as many of these methods the company chooses to use should lead to a decision on each candidate's suitability for telecommuting. The decision can be that of one or more people—the telecommuting committee, a person responsible for telecommuting, the telecommuter candidate, the supervisor, or someone else. It can be formalized with points for various "good answers" and cut-offs that eliminate the candidate from the program. It can even be totally informal, with all the data helping to produce a gut feeling that this candidate has a good chance of success, whereas someone else does not. However, some type of selection process is critical because from this point on employees' expectations will be much greater, and they will perceive failure to become a telecommuter as failure at their job. The company will also have a much larger stake in the success of those who have been selected because the expenditure of resources on them for training and home office setup will be much greater.

# Appendix A

# Questions and Answers From Homemade Telecommuting Surveys

## Questions

1. Do you have a space in your house where you can have quiet and be free from interruptions?

2. Do you find yourself often interrupted at work by people with unexpected questions or demands?

3. Are you more comfortable meeting with people to solve problems or doing the solving on your own?

4. Does your job require you to meet with other people often?

5. Do your job activities allow you to create milestones, times for products to be delivered, and other measurable criteria of completion?

6. Would you consider yourself a procrastinator or a person who gets right at it?

7. Would you rather have someone to consult with as you develop your work schedule, or do you prefer to do it on your own?

## Answers and Scoring (for self-scoring process)

1. _____ This is an important question. If you can't answer honestly that you have a place in your home that is quiet and in which you can shut yourself off, then you will probably have a difficult time with telecommuting. *Give yourself 5 points for a yes and 0 for a no.*

2. _____ One advantage of telecommuting is that when you're away from the office you are away from the passersby who drop in and say, "Hey, have you got a minute?" *If you receive unexpected interruptions (the boss doesn't count) more than five times in an average day, give yourself 5 points. If it happens at least twice a day, give yourself 2 points.*

3. _____ People who like to brainstorm or walk down the hall to talk a problem over with someone else (and become one of those unexpected interruptions) have a more difficult time telecommuting because they don't have that ability at home. *Give yourself 5 points if you said "solving on your own."*

4. _____ If your job requires a lot of meetings, particularly with people who are hard to schedule meetings with, telecommuting may be difficult for you. *Give yourself a 5 if you said no, 0 if you said yes, and 2 if you do so occasionally.*

5. _____ This is another make-it-or-break-it question. Good telecommuting demands that work can be easily evaluated and that it has plenty of places for checkpoints and the ability to create a timeline to follow toward completion. This lets you and your supervisor know how you're doing when you call in. *Give yourself a 5 if your work can be cut up into measurable chunks, a 0 if it cannot.*

6. _____ Procrastination is one of the deadly vices of telecommuting. You need to develop the discipline to get down to work and do it. *If you have a tendency to procrastinate or need a push to get going, give yourself a 0. If you only procrastinate on little things, you can have a 1. If you never procrastinate and think you deserve a 5, give yourself a 3 because nobody is perfect, and modesty is a good virtue to cultivate in a telecommuter.*

7. _____ Being responsible for planning your work schedule and to-do lists is an important part of telecommuting. If you usually ask for help in areas such as prioritizing, organization, or developing work plans, you may have problems with

telecommuting. *Give yourself a 5 if you are a self-planner who likes to develop your own way of doing things. Give yourself a 2 if you usually look to your supervisor to provide planning and prioritizing support. Give yourself a 0 if your spouse does these things for you.*

# Appendix B

# MadLib-Style Excerpt

## How Telecommuters Spend Their Day

On my _____ (a number 1-5) telecommuting days each week, I usually get started about _____ (a time of day), when I get out of bed. I usually dress in _____ (an article of clothing) and _____ (another article of clothing) because I like to strike a balance between comfort and getting too sloppy.

By _____ (a time of day), the family is gone or taken care of, and I begin my day by settling into my office which is located near the _____ (an area of the house). I have a morning routine in which the first thing I do is to _____ (physical action) the office. Next I check my _____ (noun...thing) and then read my _____ (noun...thing).

Checking on my daily to-do list is an _____ (adjective) part of my day. I try to keep it at no more than _____ (a number between 1 and 100) items to keep from feeling overloaded. I also have _____ (period of time) and _____ (period of time) planning lists that I review, shifting items from list to list, and adding others as needed. This is also the time I check for _____ (noun...thing) that may be coming due, and when my next _____ (noun...thing) with my _____ (noun...person) is planned.

The family starts to arrive home around _____ (time of day...p.m.), but they all know I'm not to be bothered unless it's an emergency until _____ (later time of day...p.m.).

My schedule normally finds me ending work by _____ (time of day... p.m.) unless I'm involved with a project deadline. I've found that without a normal quitting time, I'd work till _____ (old saying that means a long time).

My end of the day ritual includes updating my _____ (noun...thing), _____ (verb) any last minute _____(plural noun), and _____(-ing verb). To prepare for tomorrow, if it's going to be another telecommuting day, I make a _____(adjective) call to the _____ (noun...place). If I'm going to the office, I make sure I pack my _____ (noun...thing) and make a _____ (adjective) check of my needed-from-the-office lists.

The last thing I do is _____ (verb) my computer, and then I'm home, except I didn't have to get in the _____ (noun...thing) and _____ (verb) my way there.

# Appendix C

# Example of Checklists

## Personal Traits Checklist

- [ ] I'm good at organization.
- [ ] I can set goals and meet them.
- [ ] I can develop schedules and stick to them.
- [ ] I can deal with the isolation of telecommuting.
- [ ] I can deal well with distractions.
- [ ] I can work well with a minimum of supervision.
- [ ] I can communicate well using technologies such as phones, fax, and e-mail.
- [ ] I'm self-motivated and don't tend toward procrastination.
- [ ] I'm flexible.
- [ ] I'm not a workaholic.
- [ ] I'm good at meeting deadlines.
- [ ] I'm a competent time manager.
- [ ] Roadblocks do not demotivate me.
- [ ] I don't need other people's input to make decisions.
- [ ] I'm a good stress manager.

## Work Space Checklist

- [ ] I have a private space in which to set up my home office.
- [ ] It has the necessary space.
- [ ] I meet the necessary power and lighting requirements.
- [ ] I have the furniture I need.
- [ ] There is one or more phone connections.

- [ ] There is storage space in my office or near it.
- [ ] I have a good comfortable chair.
- [ ] Ventilation, heating, and cooling are good in my office space.
- [ ] My computer screen can be positioned to minimize glare.
- [ ] My office will pass a safety check.

## Personal Advantages and Disadvantages Checklist

### Advantages
- [ ] No commuting.
- [ ] More time for my family.
- [ ] More flexibility for child or elder care.
- [ ] Freedom to work when most productive.
- [ ] Greater job satisfaction.
- [ ] Dressing down.
- [ ] Greater privacy.
- [ ] Fewer interruptions.
- [ ] Fewer meetings.
- [ ] Nicer working environment.

### Disadvantages
- [ ] Isolation.
- [ ] Problems with those who live at home.
- [ ] Loss of office opportunities because not there.
- [ ] Always being at work.
- [ ] Poorer communications.
- [ ] Co-worker jealousy.
- [ ] Lost office services.
- [ ] Loss of grapevine.
- [ ] Falling into bad habits at home.
- [ ] Never leaving the office environment.

## Home Life Checklist

☐ I've talked about telecommuting with my spouse, and he or she supports it.

☐ I've talked about telecommuting with the rest of the family, and they understand what it does and doesn't mean.

☐ I'm not planning to use telecommuting as a substitute for child care or elder care.

☐ My friends and neighbors will respect the fact that even though I'm home, I'm working.

☐ I can ignore my housework chores when I'm doing my telecommuting work.

☐ I'm not trying to use telecommuting to solve already existing family problems by being home more.

☐ My family is willing to give up a room so it can be my office.

☐ My older children understand that when they come home from school it doesn't mean I'm home from work.

☐ My family's schedule and my work schedule will be compatible.

☐ I can stop personal errands from putting me off track.

## Personal Job Analysis

☐ My chances for advancement will not suffer if I telecommute.

☐ I do not require office machines and support systems in my job that cannot be duplicated in my home office.

☐ I can group necessary office tasks for planned office days.

☐ My boss and I have a good relationship.

☐ I get along well with my co-workers.

☐ My job does not rely on in-person contact.

☐ My job does not require constant feedback or input from co-workers.

☐ My work objectives are clear and measurable.

☐ My job requires heavy concentration.

☐ I normally don't have projects with short notice or short turn-around times.

☐ My work group seldom needs ad hoc meetings.

- [ ] I've been on the job long enough to know it and the organization.
- [ ] My job tasks allow for the development of recognizable mile-stones.
- [ ] On-the-job travel can begin and end as easily at home as at the office.
- [ ] Security of information concerns for my job can be addressed in the home environment.

# 7

# Training Telecommuters

*"Have an end of the day ritual so you can turn off."*
— Experienced Telecommuter

The selection methods should discern employees who have the right stuff to become successful telecommuters. This chapter will describe how to develop a training program that will allow them to reach their full telecommuting potential.

By the time candidates are ready to begin a training program, they are for all practical purposes telecommuters. They have been through the orientation that introduced them to telecommuting and the selection process that helped them and others determine if they would make good telecommuters, and they have had themselves, their job, and their department analyzed to the point at which everyone has decided that they are capable of functioning successfully in a telecommuting environment. The purpose of the training program is to make them the most effective telecommuters possible.

## A Telecommuter Training Design

There are numerous ways to design a telecommuter training program and just about as many ways to implement one. The general design described below combines concepts that have worked for other organizations. Following the description are various implementation strategies.

## Objectives

The first step in any training design is to determine the trainee-centered objectives for the program. These objectives, made up of the program and supporting objectives, form the framework for the program and tell the trainees what they have to master to become successful telecommuters. Following is a typical style for program objectives for telecommuters:

- Program objective: At the end of this program, the trainees will be able to formulate a personal plan for telecommuting.
- Supporting objectives: To help you achieve the program objective, you will learn to:
  1. discuss the concept of telecommuting.
  2. compare telecommuting to other nontraditional work processes.
  3. describe your own organizations' definition of telecommuting.
  4. compare the advantages and disadvantages of telecommuting as they relate to organizations, employees, and the community.
  5. discuss the company's general procedures for telecommuting.
  6. determine how you will develop a proper telecommuting work space in your home.
  7. consider your hardware requirements and determine what office equipment you would like to have.
  8. discuss the supervisor's role and responsibilities in telecommuting.
  9. effectively complete a telecommuting contract.

Writing objectives, particularly ones that are trainee centered, is not an easy task—it is almost an art form. The company's training department can help develop objectives properly. It is important to spend some time on them to do them well.

## Vision and Definition

The first element in the training program should be a discussion of the telecommuting vision and definition. The participants learned a little about them during their telecommuting orientation, but this time the person leading the training can provide more detail about how these items will affect them now that they are about to become telecommuters.

Reviewing some of the thinking that went into the development of the initiative is a good approach here as well. The trainer can discuss the other types of nontraditional work processes that were explored during the analysis and show the participants how telecommuting is related to them. This stage should end with an explanation of why the committee chose telecommuting as the best intervention for the corporate environment.

### Advantages and Disadvantages

There was some discussion of advantages and disadvantages during the orientation and the selection process, but not in the detail that is now appropriate. Most of the attention now should be spent on the advantages and disadvantages from the telecommuters' point of view, but some mention should be made of telecommuting's effect on the organization and community as well. It's a good idea to use the list from the analysis in various ways during the training.

This kind of review will help set the stage for everything else that occurs during the training program. Most of the subsequent training will be concerned with methods for making the most of the advantages and moderating the disadvantages.

It could be helpful for the participants to spend some time creating a list of telecommuting's advantages and disadvantages to them. They can use this list as the training unfolds to keep a record of ideas they want to implement to make themselves more effective telecommuters.

## Characteristics of Successful Telecommuters

Trainers should focus next on suitability for telecommuting, which employees learned about during the selection process. The aim is to help participants predict trouble spots they may encounter as telecommuters and give them ideas for alleviating them.

If the company used a psychological instrument of some type (such as the preference pair instruments described in chapter 6), trainers should elaborate on it. This is the time to explain, for example, that a high score on one aspect of a pair might indicate that an employee would have problems in a telecommuting environment and how to lessen those problems. Trainers should provide details about homemade surveys or checklists that their companies used in the selection process as well.

Companies that did not use these tools during the selection process should use them now. (Sample questions are available in appendix 6A.) Excerpts from three characteristics assessment tools appear in appendix A at the end of this chapter. The concepts covered in these tools are similar to those exemplified in chapter 6, but that is as it should be. Selection and this part of the training program serve the same purpose: to provide ways for telecommuters to analyze their strengths and weaknesses in a telecommuting environment.

To save time during training, participants can complete new surveys or checklists as prework so they can concentrate on discussing them during the session. It is helpful to distribute job aids on which the participants can record the traits and characteristics that are their strengths and those upon which they will need to improve as they grow as telecommuters.

Another technique that works well is to break participants into small groups that discuss how to deal with problems isolated by the instruments. The small groups report their ideas back to the class as a whole. To save time, trainers can assign each group a different category of problems. The training department or a good telecommuting consultant can help develop these activities to their full effectiveness.

## Policies and Procedures

The greater part of the telecommuter training will focus on policies and procedures that affect telecommuters. Because the training and policies and procedures follow each other so closely, it should now be clear why chapter 4 put such a heavy emphasis on developing effective and complete policies and procedures. They guide the telecommuters now, when they need it most, and help them to make fewer mistakes, and they also make the job of the telecommuting implementer much easier. With well-thought-out policies and procedures, the implementer can develop most of the telecommuter training fairly quickly and have answers for most questions that occur during it. In fact, during planning for the training, omissions from the policies and procedures may become clear, or it may be evident that something doesn't quite work. Now is the time to make the additions and changes, before they create a problem.

The most efficient approach to this part of training is to ask the telecommuters to read the policies and procedures before class and then to answer their questions. However, it's a good idea to address first any procedures that are different from those of the corporate norm or any that are particularly difficult to understand. This reading and questioning process is a general introduction to telecommuting's policies and procedures and a means to alleviate any initial confusion by answering the participants' questions. The core of the process follows.

Some trainers might be concerned that this method won't provide trainees with all the necessary information. However, most of the class time that follows is spent dealing with these procedures, so any information omitted from the participants' questions can be filled in later.

## The Telecommuting Contract

A discussion of the organization's telecommuting contract should follow that of the general telecommuting policies and procedures. It's a good idea to go over each point of the contract with the participants because it makes a good organizer for the material to come. Because contracts differ with different organizations, the presentations will differ. A couple of telecommuting contracts are in appendix B at the end of this chapter. They may help companies in developing their own.

## Setting up the Home Office

The training program now gets into the nitty gritty of telecommuting. Companies should have some policies and procedures concerning how to get started in telecommuting and who is responsible for what office furniture and equipment. The trainer should weave those policies and procedures into a discussion of how telecommuters should get their offices up and running. Aspects to cover include the following:

- the amount of space necessary
- privacy
- security
- furniture
- lighting
- electricity
- noise
- work surface.

Some companies develop a guide or kit for planning and implementing the home office. Such kits include information on how to do office planning, diagrams of efficient office setups, checklists, hints, thoughts on furniture, and ergonomic considerations. They may include articles, ideas about how to set up your office from experienced telecommuters, and even a bibliography to help in finding more information.

Companies that use kits should also hold a class discussion during training, but they can base it on the kit, and thus make it a lot shorter.

An effective activity is to break the participants into small groups and have each group develop its own checklist for setting up a home office based on the organization's policies and procedures. The groups then present their checklists to the whole group, which then prepares one combined checklist developed from the group's best ideas.

It is important to remember that this activity is no longer just theory. The participants will be going out and creating their own office, probably in the not too distant future. They need information to help them do that well.

## Obtaining and Using Technical Equipment

Training will focus on two aspects of technology: how to get the equipment and how to use it.

The policies and procedures have most of the information they'll need for the section on getting the equipment. The discussion should contain information on the amount of lead time that will be involved as well as who is responsible for what, including repair and replacement. The trainers should also cover the use of personal equipment and the advantages and disadvantages of using their own, such as what happens if something breaks.

It is helpful to design an activity that allows each telecommuter to determine what technical equipment he or she may need in the home office. Some effective approaches include small-group brainstorming sessions in which participants describe what equipment they'd like to have and what they need to have; and sessions in which they describe the daily life of a telecommuter, comparing what they need to have to perform certain activities with what they do have.

Some of this equipment may not be listed in the policies and procedures, so getting telecommuters to think about it now can help them be more efficient later. Equipment may be items their departments will provide or they have to buy, including shredders, scanners, surge protectors, cordless phones, head sets, fax modems, and antistatic mats.

Instruction in the use of technological equipment is outside the responsibility of this training, although the training program is a good place to determine if skill deficiencies exist and who might have them. However, if a participant is deficient in technology-based skills like keyboarding, calling into the corporate LAN, using company software programs, sending a fax, and placing conference calls, I would question why he or she was selected to be a telecommuter. One way to do so is with a written or performance checklist or even with a written examination. The trainer should know what resources are available to help those who are analyzed as having skill gaps and can even do some prescriptive work with them during breaks or after the class. If there are only a few weaknesses, the best place to cover them is in a class specifically developed for that purpose.

The focus of telecommuter training for technology use, though, is more typically general concepts that might affect all the participants such as obtaining passwords, making conference calls, or dealing with a particular software glitch.

## Working as a Telecommuter

This section of the training covers the nontechnical skills a telecommuter needs in the telecommuting environment. Some of these came up when the trainers administered the instruments, surveys, or checklists. This aspect of the training should expand where necessary on these concepts and introduce any others. Following are some of the important topics to cover:
- organization
    —using objectives to manage work
    —knowing priorities
    —planning what to accomplish each day
    —establishing a daily routine
    —longer range planning for task completion

- scheduling time
  - —the importance of getting up on time
  - —making proper to-do lists
  - —following schedules
  - —learning to say no to time wasters
- planning office visits
  - —keeping a running list of what is needed from the office
  - —making appointments to talk to those it's necessary to talk to
  - —checking office schedules to match visits with important events
  - —leaving schedules of office visits
- pushing oneself
  - —setting goals and deadlines and staying with them
  - —planning little rewards
  - —reviewing the day to acknowledge accomplishments
- dealing with distractions
  - —neighbors who drop in or call for help
  - —family schedules and phone calls
  - —household chores
  - —snacks, TV, and other bad habits
  - —keeping nonwork issues out of the work area
- maintaining visibility
  - —attending important meetings and social gatherings
  - —talking to the supervisor on a scheduled basis
  - —using weekly status reports to the supervisor and others
- communicating with others in the department regularly
  - —keeping available communications hours at the home office
  - —asking for help, even when he or she doesn't particularly need it
  - —using voice mail and call forwarding
  - —keeping receptionists informed
- communicating with technology
  - —writing proper e-mail messages
  - —sounding the best on the phone

—leaving effective phone messages

—running a conference call to best effect

—running a videoconference

—rules for good faxes

—using the corporation's groupware properly and effectively

- managing stress and isolation

—using end-of-day rituals

—pacing oneself (one day's work in one day)

—going to sleep on time

—using planned interaction breaks

—the importance of having lunch and taking breaks

—using some of the extra time gained not commuting as personal time

- dealing with family

—discussing telecommuting with the family

—setting up rules for office privacy

—dealing with preschool children

—dealing with elder care

—dealing with school-aged children and their schedules

—reinforcing the fact that he or she is working even if it's at home

—setting family rules regarding interruptions

—confronting problems

- battling procrastination

—getting hated tasks out of the way first

—chunking tasks and doing a little at a time

—refusing to fall prey to time-wasting behaviors

—timing breaks and alternate task behaviors.

Some of the subtopics are applicable to more than one category, and others are closely related. The context in which the trainer covers these concepts is not as important as that they be covered. The telecommuters will decide for themselves where these subtopics fit best, as long as they have been stimulated to think about them.

A method I've used with success for this area is the Day in the Life type of telecommuting simulation described in chapter 6. It is an effective activity for learning what a telecommuter should be doing and can be put to use here even if it was used in the selection process. The entire class or small groups should discuss how a telecommuter goes through a normal day of telecommuting, bringing in the items on the foregoing list.

## The Supervisor's Role

The supervisor is critical to the telecommuter's success, so it is important to discuss that role in detail. In most telecommuting interventions, the direct supervisor will already be involved in the process at some level.

The goal is for the telecommuter to understand the importance of the supervisor's role and the problems the supervisor might be facing. This area should go into depth on ways to communicate, performance measurements, and the development of trust as a two-way street. Special emphasis should be on dealing with co-workers who are not telecommuting.

Two methods—a structured role play and questions—provide effective training about the supervisor's role. In a structured role play, participants take on both the telecommuter and supervisor roles. One approach is to base the role play around the telecommuting contract, perhaps through a simulation of a meeting at which the supervisor and telecommuter fill out and agree to the contract. This method also helps to make the participants more familiar with the contract.

I've used an observer to form a triad for the role play if I have enough class time and have rotated the roles of the supervisor and telecommuter to allow each participant to play both parts. The observer looks for behaviors each person should exhibit and then describes the role play. It is effective to have each group mention one or two behaviors that came out of the role play, and it's a good idea to include a sheet with the participant materials for trainees to note items of personal interest to them in this area.

The second method is a series of questions concerning telecommuting based on the supervisor's perspective. These can be answered individually or better still in small groups, and then discussed by the class as a whole. Following are examples of some of these questions:

1. What responsibilities do supervisors have in supporting the telecommuter?
2. How can the supervisor and telecommuter ensure good communications?
3. What approaches can the supervisor follow in assigning and measuring work for a telecommuter?
4. What are the best ways for the supervisor to measure the telecommuter's performance?
5. How should the supervisor and telecommuter discuss the process of telecommuting with team co-workers who are not telecommuting?
6. By what methods can the supervisor and telecommuter develop a sense of trust in each other?

It is important to note that the training program is for telecommuters, but that does not mean that the supervisors cannot and should not attend. I've had my greatest success with telecommuting when the supervisors were interested enough in the process to find out what their telecommuters were learning about. Attendance here does not, however, take the place of the supervisor's telecommuting training, which is covered in the next chapter, although much of the introductory material is the same for both groups.

Supervisors who are committed enough and have the time should attend the telecommuter training as well as their own. If they can't, I suggest they go to the section on the supervisor's role. The role plays will be a lot more interesting and effective if the supervisors are actually taking part. Some reverse role playing would also be effective—and maybe even illuminating. I once had a client tell me that the supervisors would not be comfortable attending a class with their telecommuters, let alone doing reverse role plays. Companies in which that's the case should look once more at the whole concept of telecommuting, even at this late point in the process. My client, who was soon not a client, certainly did.

## Implementation Strategies

The approach in this chapter has been that telecommuter training would be in a classroom. Although this is usually the case, it is not necessarily the rule. Chapter 6 mentioned a computer-mediated instruction format using a combined telephone and computer network to give the telecommuting candidates some idea of what it is like to telecommute. This is also a valid approach for telecommuter training in general. In fact, the first time I used this technology was for training, not selection. Because it is real-time interactive, with a few modifications most of the classroom approach can be implemented with this technology as well.

The advantage of this method is that it can also simulate the telecommuting environment by having the participants conference call (work in small groups), manipulate files (report back), and basically perform many of the activities that they would do in a normal day of telecommuting. I'd recommend this approach if you have the technology or can lease it. It is particularly efficient for large corporations that want to start telecommuters at a number of locations simultaneously. It is also extremely cost-effective in these environments or in small but highly dispersed companies such as sales organizations.

Companies may want to consider using a satellite-mediated distance-learning methodology for telecommuter training implementation. This is normally more expensive than the computer-mediated technology, but it does present more possibilities for interaction. Some companies can lease not only the equipment but also the facility, and even instructors, to facilitate this approach. With this approach, companies won't have to expend capital for technology they need for telecommuter training but might not use too often.

Although I have used some individualized technology implementations to good effect for prework aspects of telecommuter training, particularly in the areas that deal mostly with policies and procedures, I don't recommend using them for the rest of the process. Telecommuter training requires interaction, responses sometimes to off-the-wall questions, and the human feeling that these technologies can't deliver. Real-time face-to-face contact must be part of your program, even if it's through a computer or a satellite.

## Hints

I like to complete my telecommuter training with what I call hints from experienced telecommuters. Usually I project them for the class to see and record if they strike home. I ask questions like the following: "Why do you think this telecommuter would say that," or "What did you learn today that would help you deal with that"? The hints also make a pretty good summary of some of the major issues and let the telecommuters know that they are not really out there alone. Others have gone before them and experienced similar problems, and there are resources to go to for help when they have problems. I've listed some of my favorite hints here. You may recognize some of them as quotes that opened each of the chapters.

- "Learn to say no when you need to."
- "Get plenty of sleep."
- "Learn to solve problems right away."
- "When you've finished for the day, turn off your phone—and your mind."
- "If you spend time on the road, let the office know how you can be reached."
- "Take home more work than you think you'll need, because you never know."

- "Right from the start communicate your work needs with family and friends."
- "Don't become invisible!"
- "If it feels right, it probably is."
- "Many of your hoped for advantages can be a double-edged sword."
- "It's not a cure for a bad family life, in fact it will probably make it worse."
- "Plan breaks and then take them when they're planned."
- "Have an end-of-day ritual so you can turn off."

## Summary of Creating a Telecommuter Training Program

Following is a checklist of the elements that are important to cover when creating a telecommuter training program:

☐ Definition of telecommuting
☐ Contrast of telecommuting to other alternative officing processes
☐ Company's definition of telecommuting
☐ Advantages and disadvantages of telecommuting for employees, company, and the community at large
☐ Company's purposes in supporting the process of telecommuting
☐ Psychological appropriateness for telecommuting
☐ Environmental, physical, and work factors that affect telecommuters
☐ Comparison of own personal traits and commitments to standards that are necessary for a telecommuter
☐ General procedures for telecommuting
☐ Development of a proper telecommuting work space
☐ Analysis of hardware needs and how to meet those needs
☐ The supervisor's role and responsibilities in a telecommuting environment
☐ Development of a plan to make telecommuting a success

# Appendix A

# Excerpts from Assessment Tools

### The Telecommuter's Skills

A variety of general skills are important for telecommuters in most telecommuting situations. Following is a skill list for assessing telecommuting candidates:

- The candidate's experience in the company. *(Successful telecommuters have usually been with the company long enough to know its basic policies and have a solid infrastructure.)*
- The candidate's basic job skills and knowledge of position. *(Telecommuting is not the place to receive on-the-job training.)*
- Planning skills. *(This includes to-do lists and long-range planning.)*
- Time-management skills. *(This includes planning when to start and stop working.)*
- Communications skills. *(The telecommuter listens well and gets messages across.)*
- Basic computer skills. *(The telecommuter knows how to use the necessary hardware and general software.)*
- Voice mail. *(This includes accessing it and using it to leave coherent messages.)*

### The Telecommuter's Home Environment

The family and the overall home situation play a large part in the success or failure of individual telecommuters. The following concepts have proved to be critical environmental factors:

- The telecommuter needs a basically sound family life with no pivotal problems. *(Telecommuting is likely to exacerbate what is already wrong.)*
- Telecommuting should not be seen as a solution to child- or elder-care difficulties. *(It is effective in emergencies, but not on a day-to-day basis.)*
- The family will need to understand the reason for privacy and provide it as required. *(The work space needs to be the domain of the telecommuter, not a family gathering place.)*
- Work space lighting should be good. *(A ceiling light is seldom enough.)*
- There should be a separate temperature control or mechanism in the work space. *(This is for the comfort of others and cost savings on utilities.)*
- Sufficient outlets and proper wiring should be part of the work space.
- The work space will need telephone outlets.

## General Telecommuter Attributes

**There seem to be psychological characteristics and attributes that give a telecommuter a better chance at being successful. Following is a list of general attributes for assessing candidates for telecommuting.**

- Self-motivated
- Self-disciplined
- Flexible
- Comfortable working where he or she lives. *(Telecommuting can lead to cabin fever or a reclusive existence in extremes.)*
- Does not require a lot of input from others
- Is comfortable with minimal supervision *(Telecommuting can actually increase the level of supervision, but a good telecommuter will not need it if it doesn't.)*
- Self-evaluatory *(Knows when he or she has done a job well)*

# Appendix B

# Examples of Telecommuting Contracts

## Telecommuting Contract (Supervisor/Telecommuter)

The two of us agree to work as a team to make telecommuting a success.

- We will carefully define measurable objectives and valid time frames for completing them in a telecommuting environment.
- We will communicate on a scheduled basis with each other and with colleagues in the office.
- We will give and receive feedback on projects and problems on a scheduled basis.
- We will develop trust and commitment to each other and to the project.

The following are the objectives to be accomplished in this first contract period:

1. The measurement of completion for each objective is:

2. The schedule of completion for each objective is:

3. The telecommuter's hours of availability will be (this should not change unless everyone is notified):

4. The telecommuter's core days in the office will be:

5. The telecommuter's communication plan with the office is:

6. The communication plan between telecommuter and supervisor is:

7. The plan for dealing with the telecommuter's office mail is:

8. The plan for dealing with the telecommuter's phone messages is:

9. The plan for communicating telecommuting process with the rest of work group and keeping telecommuter part of group is:

10. The date for next review of this contract is:

# Telecommuting Contract

This document is an agreement between _____ (employee) and _____ (supervisor) in regard to a telecommuting work arrangement, that includes work schedule, equipment used, and other details.

It will begin the week of _____ (dates).

1.  The employee will work off-site at _____ (location).

2.  The employee will telecommute according to the following schedule:

3.  The employee will provide the following equipment at the home office site:

4.  The employee will need to have the following equipment provided by the company and installed at the home office site:

5.  When working off-site, the employee will keep in touch with his or her supervisor according to the following schedule:

6.  When working off-site, the employee will keep in touch with his or her co-workers at the office in the following ways:

7.  The employee will focus on the following work tasks when working from home:

8.  The employee's additional telephone line, the monthly connection costs, long-distance charges, plus any special services (call waiting, call forwarding, voice mail, etc.) will be paid for as follows:

9.  The supervisor will determine the employee's productivity through these processes (number of phone calls, pages read or written, hours spent working, milestones met, etc.):

10. The employee will participate in meetings and conferences held in the office in his or her absence through (teleconferencing, video conferencing, the receipt of minutes, etc.):

11. The employee and supervisor will meet _____ to monitor the telecommuting arrangement.

12. Other aspects of this contract are:

| | |
|---|---|
| _____ | ___ / ___ / ___ |
| Employee Signature | Date |
| _____ | ___ / ___ / ___ |
| Supervisor Signature | Date |

## Telecommuting Contract

When this telecommuting arrangement is implemented, the following conditions will apply:

1. The employee's salary, job responsibilities, benefits, and company-sponsored insurance coverage will not change due to participation in the telecommuting project.

2. The amount of time the employee is expected to work will not change due to participation in the telecommuting project.

3. The employee's work hours will conform to a schedule agreed upon by the telecommuter and his or her manager for compensation and HR purposes.

4. The employee will telecommute _____ days per (week, month). Changes to this must be prearranged with the supervisor.

5. Any changes that affect compensation or HR claims must be reviewed and approved in advance by a member of management.

6. The remote work location will be:

Street address _____

City _____State _____Zip code_____

Phone _____Fax _____

E-mail _____

7. As the employee's home work space will be considered an extension of the company work space, the company's liability for job-related accidents will continue to exist during the understood and approved job hours.

8. A designated work space will be maintained by the telecommuter at the alternate work location with proper privacy and security arrangements. Workers' compensation liability will be limited to this work space as opposed to applying to all areas of the home.

9. The employer may make on-site inspections of this work area to ensure that safe work conditions exist. These inspections are to be prearranged at a time agreed upon by the telecommuter.

10. The employer may also enter the house for the purpose of repairing or retrieving equipment and other company property in the event of employee illness or termination, again at a time agreed to by the employee.

11. Any hardware or software purchased by the company remains the property of the company and will be returned to the company at the conclusion of the telecommuting period. Company equipment at the remote location will not be used for personal purposes except under the following circumstances:

    The following equipment will be lent to the telecommuter:

12. Restricted-access materials (such as payroll) shall not be taken out of the main office or accessed through the computer at a remote location except in the following circumstances:

13. The company will provide the following furniture for the home office:

14. The telecommuter will provide the following equipment for the home office:

15. The company will reimburse the telecommuter for the following telephone expenses:

16. The company will supply materials necessary to complete assigned work at the alternate location through the telecom-

muter's in-office visits. Out-of-pocket expenses for supplies normally available through the company will not be reimbursed.

17. If the telecommuter has school-aged or younger children at home, child-care arrangements have been made for the agreed-upon work hours.

I, the telecommuter, understand the terms of this telecommuting agreement and agree to the responsibilities and conditions for telecommuters expressed herein.

_____     __ / __ / __

Employee Signature                          Date

# 8

# Training Telecommuter Supervisors

---

*"If you and your supervisor don't trust each other, don't telecommute!"*

—Experienced Telecommuter

---

A successful telecommuting process is comprised of the organization, the telecommuter, and the supervisor. This chapter explores the role of the supervisor in telecommuting, and how he or she should be prepared for that role.

## Why Supervisor Training?

Many companies' experiences indicate that the number one cause of failure in telecommuting initiatives pertains to the telecommuters' supervisor. Supervisors can make or break a telecommuting program before it ever gets off the ground, simply by the way they react to the initial publicity surrounding the process. It is essential to have their support in sending interested staff members to the orientation meeting and in recommending them as suitable for telecommuting. How they help prepare employees for telecommuting and how they manage them once they are in a telecommuting role are critical factors in the success of the initiative.

Their role is so crucial that they require their own training program to prepare them for telecommuting. This training should cover at least some of the following:

- definition of telecommuting
- advantages and disadvantages
- characteristics of a successful telecommuter
- management problems associated with telecommuting
- necessary management skills
- communications and trust
- the telecommuting contract
- managers' fears
- preparation and training for those left behind.

The following sections describe these important elements of supervisor training.

## Definition

The supervisors need to discuss telecommuting in much the same way as the organization and the telecommuters themselves did. Supervisors need to consider what is and isn't telecommuting, how telecommuting relates to other nontraditional work processes, and, of course, how the organization's definition relates to these concepts. The purpose of this segment of training is to explore the supervisors' preconceived notions of telecommuting and introduce them to the company's position.

## Advantages and Disadvantages

This discussion of the pros and cons of training should explore the supervisors' positive and negative feelings about telecommuting, the assumptions they have, and the myths they believe. It should also look at the advantages and disadvantages they might not have considered. Someone who was present at the meetings at which the organization deliberated about telecommuting should review those talks.

A discussion of the telecommuting vision as put forth by the organization in the policies and procedures and its overall effects on supervision come next. That talk leads into a discussion of the company's general telecommuting policies and procedures. Specific policies and procedures as they relate to the managers will be covered later, but this is the place to talk about how telecommuting will work in the organization and the managers' overall role in the process.

These first two segments (and a couple of others that will be discussed later) are closely aligned with material in the orientation and training programs. If supervisors and managers are included in the orientation meetings, the first topic can be scaled down considerably for the supervisors' training. Better yet, if supervisors are required to attend at least one of the telecommuters' training programs, both of the previous segments as well as others that follow can be shortened.

There are pros and cons for requiring supervisors to attend the orientation and telecommuters' programs, and each company must make its own decisions based on organizational needs and culture. Because it's important for supervisors to know as much as possible about the organization's telecommuting processes, I usually recommend that the orientation meeting be mandatory for every supervisor and manager and that supervisors who will have telecommuters reporting to them be required to attend at least one iteration of the telecommuters' training program. Among other advantages, this approach makes it possible to condense the supervisors' training.

However, because some organizations may not wish to go this route, this chapter describes supervisors' training as if it were the main information source. It also points out where it is possible to cut information.

### Characteristics of a Successful Telecommuter

This segment provides information supervisors need to effectively recommend individuals for the telecommuting process. However, even if a supervisory recommendation is not part of a company's procedures, a knowledge of the characteristics that can make or possibly undo a telecommuter will benefit supervisors as they manage telecommuters.

Topics that should receive consideration include the psychological aspects, including whatever instrument or survey the company has chosen for determining telecommuting suitability; environmental aspects such as space for a home office; family support; technological ability; position characteristics such as work portability; and ability to get things done with reduced support structures. Any checklists, simulations, or other written activities that were used in the orientation and telecommuters' training to cover these topics will be useful here as well.

If the supervisors attended these other training processes, trainers could abridge this discussion, but they should not delete it because even a review of these aspects will make the attendees better supervisors of telecommuters.

## Management Problems Associated With Telecommuting

This segment continues the discussion of advantages and disadvantages begun earlier, but deals specifically with supervisory disadvantages. The discussion should focus on the problems inherent with supervising individuals who aren't seen on a daily basis, sometimes referred to as remote management. Trainers can divide this segment into three major areas: personal problems of telecommuters, direct supervisory problems, and office mechanics problems.

The first area looks at the problems telecommuters often have adjusting to telecommuting. Their problems might include loss of interaction with other people, tendencies to overwork, inability to find the discipline to work alone, feelings of being left out, family problems, and other psychological pressures that are inherent in telecommuting. Supervisors need to be made aware of these possible problems, discuss how to spot them, and share ideas on how to deal with them when they arise.

The second area deals with problems associated with what would be normal day-to-day supervision. These include communicating with the telecommuter, monitoring productivity, in some environments monitoring work hours, and basic control problems.

These and other related topics should be identified as problems in this segment and then dealt with in the next segment on skills for managing telecommuters. Trainers will find it effective to keep a list of the problems the supervisors identify in this section and then refer to them during the segment that follows on necessary management skills.

The third area includes problems associated with the mechanics of telecommuting. Some of the critical concepts to address are office availability, missed meetings, material not available at home, scheduling of phone calls, technology support, inability to switch projects rapidly, schedule coordination, and most important, relationships with work group members who remain in the office.

A number of these topics relate directly to a company's telecommuting policies and procedures. These should receive as specific review as applicable. Others are management skill related, and as such are discussed in more detail in the next segment. Telecommuters' relationship with work-group members receives special consideration during discussion of the preparation and training of employees who remain in the office.

## Management Skills Necessary for Successful Telecommuting

The trainer now addresses the skills necessary to deal with the disadvantages and problems brought up in the previous segments. Because supervisors have probably received training related to some of these skills, a brief review related directly to telecommuting should be all that is necessary. These concepts might include goal setting, development of milestones, and listening skills.

The review should focus on how proper use of these management skills will negate the disadvantages or help solve telecommuting supervisory problems. Where necessary a quick refresher of the skill itself may be in order.

Topics that probably require a more in-depth consideration include enhanced communications on a scheduled basis, monitoring work over distances, coaching employees who are not face to face with the supervisors, developing work agreements, and recognizing telecommuter problems.

These topics probably did not receive emphasis in the basic supervisors' training program. Trainers need to consider them from a skills-building or how-to approach, rather than as a refresher of the earlier topics.

Concurrent with management skills, supervisors need details about how to plan and implement the telecommuting process. Both aspects depend on the company's telecommuting policies and procedures, so trainers need to reinforce this information, but this time from a planning and implementation perspective.

Implementation is a combination of policies and procedures and good practices. Important topics to cover include keeping telecommuters on lists to receive memos and e-mail, scheduling team meetings for the telecommuters' office days, and ensuring that telecommuters do not become invisible. The group should consider concepts such as how to recognize good performance in a telecommuter, methods for bringing outstanding performance by telecommuters to upper management's attention, ways to develop individuals who are telecommuting, delegation of assignments so everyone gets a fair share of both the good and bad ones, assignment of appropriate and visible committee work to telecommuters, and job security and value issues. The key is to short circuit the out-of-sight, out-of-mind syndrome.

Finally, supervisors have to consider measurement and appraisal of telecommuters and their productivity needs. Some of the aspects of this area, such as structuring telecommuting work and setting objectives and goals, have probably been discussed earlier. They should now be combined with concepts such as developing variously timed (weekly, monthly, quarterly) task-completion lists, scheduling status reports, and how to manage by results. Discussions and role plays in which people take the parts of supervisors and telecommuters are the best instructional techniques.

## Communications and Trust

Communications and trust are two keys to successful management of telecommuters. The goal of this segment, and of the whole process of communications and trust, is to show that an effective telecommuting process is one in which there are no surprises.

Good communications lead to trust on both ends of the telecommuting phone. Ideas for communicating range from simple ones like scheduling times for phone calls to complex concepts such as monitoring how well the new telecommuter is adapting to telecommuting. The relationship of communication and trust is so critical that it should receive special consideration during the training.

In this training segment, it is important to reemphasize the coaching technique as it relates to the clarification of expectations. Trainers should explore the importance of flexibility in developing trust and of balancing communications to avoid a perception of ignoring the telecommuters, on the one hand, and falling into the trap of oversupervising, on the other. Trainers should stress the value of dealing with problems early, effectively, and as a team.

A good instructional technique for this segment is to have the managers develop a general communications plan that they will use with their telecommuters, and then to list the key aspects of their plan that will lead to developing trust.

## The Telecommuting Contract

Companies that followed the earlier recommendations about policy and procedure development will have created a telecommuting contract for telecommuters and their supervisors. Trainers review the contract in detail, explaining why each item is part of the contract and how it should be completed. Role plays can help illuminate problems that might occur when the manager and telecommuter actually work together on a contract.

Trainers should open discussion and provide advice about ways supervisors and telecommuters can work on the contract. Points to consider include scheduling enough time to produce a good contract, not filling out the contract in advance of the meeting, either physically or mentally, making completion a shared process not a led process, ensuring that the objectives and goals are achievable and the timing reasonable, and keeping the communications plan realistic. Trainers should stress the importance of this document as the foundation for successful telecommuting. Each supervisor should leave the training program with a completed contract *that he or she developed.*

This segment ends with a discussion of when and how to review and revise the contract, and the importance of not postponing this critical aspect of the contract process once dates and times are set.

This is another segment that can be shortened considerably if supervisors attend the telecommuters' training program.

## Managers' Fears

Through most of this training program, the discussion has centered around supervisory problems and telecommuters' concerns. However, managers have their own concerns about telecommuting as well. Some of the concerns, such as the loss of supervisory control and the inability to use accustomed management techniques, focus on the process. This segment of training looks at those that affect managers themselves.

Telecommuting hits managers' often unspoken concerns about job security. Managers often ask themselves, "If this catches on, and everyone becomes a telecommuter, why would they need me?" Telecommuting requires more and better management, not less. The skills are somewhat different, but hardly a stretch for someone who is already an effective supervisor.

This concern, and other fears the participants might identify in this segment, need to be discussed. If managers are having difficulty accepting their new roles, some training on how to deal with change may be in order. Any managers who agree with the supervisor whose only contribution during the training session was to adamantly declare, "Remote management isn't management!" are giving early warnings that they will likely not be successful supervisors of telecommuters.

## Preparing and Training Those Left Behind

A component of telecommuting initiatives that is easily overlooked, often with disastrous results, is the training of those employees who are not telecommuting. Because these employees form the support structure for telecommuters, their understanding and support are extremely important to the intervention's long-term viability.

How those who stay behind relate to these new "ghosts in the office"—the telecommuters who appear and disappear at various times—is basically a communications process. A well-prepared supervisor should address this issue in group meetings that both telecommuters and their in-the-office colleagues attend.

If everyone attended the telecommuting orientation program, the supervisor should review topics such as what telecommuting is, what it isn't, why are we doing it, and how the telecommuters were chosen. Other topics such as what the telecommuters will be doing, what types of support they will need, changes in meeting structure or workload distribution that may result from telecommuting, telecommuters' schedules, and how to communicate with them are specific to each individual work group and supervisor. The supervisor needs to be ready to explain these processes, answer questions, and deal with doubts.

A first meeting should take place before telecommuting begins. This timing will aid in getting the work group to support the process. Follow-ups need to be held as well, either separately or as part of scheduled team meetings, to discuss how the telecommuting process is working, and to deal with communications or other problems and perceptions.

It is important to the success of the initiative that the telecommuters not be left on their own. Preparing supervisors to prepare the work group to understand and support the process will help ensure that this does not happen.

# Summary of Training Telecommuter Supervisors

The purpose of telecommuter supervisor training is to develop managers who can help make the transition to telecommuting smooth and efficient and the process itself as effective as possible. It should create supervisors such as Laura, who defined her role as a telecommuter supervisor this way: "My responsibility is to help my telecommuters succeed, grow, and develop, the same as I do for all my staff." And it should put to rest questions such as that of one of Laura's colleagues who asked in all seriousness and confusion, "How can I justify laying off my staff who come to work every day before I lay off the telecommuters?"

Following is a checklist of important elements to include in telecommuter supervisor training:

☐ Definition
  - What telecommuting is and what it isn't
  - How it relates to other nontraditional work processes
  - The organization's definition

☐ Advantages and disadvantages
  - Advantages for employee, employer, and community
  - Disadvantages for employee, employer, and community
  - The company's telecommuting vision
  - General policies and procedures

☐ Characteristics of a successful telecommuter
  - Psychological aspects of telecommuting
  - Environmental aspects of telecommuting
  - Technological ability

☐ Management problems associated with telecommuting
  - Telecommuters' personal problems
  - Loss of interaction with other people
  - Tendencies toward overwork
  - Inability to find the discipline to work alone
  - Feelings of being left out
  - Family problems

- Direct supervisory problems
- Communicating with the telecommuter
- Monitoring productivity
- Monitoring work hours
- Basic control problems
- Office mechanics problems
- Office availability
- Missed meetings
- Scheduling of phone calls
- Technology support
- Inability to switch projects rapidly
- Schedule coordination
- Relationships with work-group members in the office

☐ Management skills necessary for successful telecommuting
- Goal setting
- Development of milestones
- Listening skills
- Enhanced communications on a scheduled basis
- Monitoring work over distances
- Coaching employees when they and supervisors are not face to face
- Developing work agreements
- Recognizing telecommuter problems
- Integrating the telecommuter with the office
- Dealing with telecommuter invisibility
- Measurement and appraisal of telecommuters and their productivity

☐ Communications and trust
- Clarification of expectations
- The importance of flexibility
- Balancing communications
- Dealing with problems early

☐ The telecommuting contract
- Scheduling enough time

- Don't do in advance
- Shared not led process
- Achievable objectives
- Reasonable timing
- Realistic communications plan
- Contract review and revision

☐ Managers' fears
- Loss of supervisory control
- Inability to use comfortable management techniques
- Job security

☐ Preparation and training of those left behind
- What telecommuting is, what it isn't, and why we are doing it
- How and why these individuals have been chosen
- What will they be doing when they are telecommuting
- What having a telecommuting colleague means and doesn't mean
- What support telecommuters need from those in the office
- How telecommuting will or will not affect in-office workers
- Changes in meeting structure or workload distribution
- Telecommuters' schedules and how to communicate with them
- Support personnel and their role
- Answering telecommuters' phone correctly (not at home or not in)
- Procedures for dealing with the problems that will come up
- Jealousy and other feelings or perceptions related to telecommuting.

# 9

# Monitoring and Evaluation

---

*"Be honest with yourself, are you happy?"*

—Experienced Telecommuter

---

It is not possible to label an organizational intervention as successful until it has been formally evaluated. This chapter describes possible forms of evaluation and ways to organize an evaluation plan that gathers relevant data as it helps telecommuters to succeed.

## Monitoring

Chapter 4 described the development of monitoring procedures, and chapter 5 mentioned that both managers and top administrators could help with the monitoring process. This chapter describes reasons for monitoring the telecommuting program, what might be monitored, and who should do it.

The first step is to decide the goals of the monitoring process. Monitoring can function as a support process for the telecommuters, a communications tool to develop continuing support for the intervention, and even as a data-gathering method for an evaluation process. Which of these goals, or any others, a company chooses depends on its particular initiative and resources.

## Monitoring to Support the Telecommuters

If one of the goals is to support the telecommuters, the monitoring should be done by someone who can be trusted to report back accurately and not create expectations that the program will not be able to fulfill. This person will be monitoring the telecommuters and possibly their supervisors directly, usually through phone conversations or visits. That person must not be too intrusive or demanding in implementing the monitoring process, and must not promise things that can't be delivered.

Monitoring that supports telecommuters should be done in a systematic fashion with a list of prepared questions and behaviors to observe. Reports should be timely and concise and should include the monitor's impressions and thoughts on what is happening and what should be done. (See appendix A.)

General questions are effective ways for monitors to gct telecommuters and their supervisors thinking during these interviews. Some questions include: "Have you reached your expected outcomes in the telecommuting environment?" and "Where do you feel we can upgrade our approach to telecommuting?" Monitors can then probe for workable solutions and recommendations.

## Monitoring as a Communications Tool

If the main purpose for monitoring is to build support through communications, a number of people at different levels of the organization should be both monitors and responders. The method that works best for this type of monitoring is informal. For this goal it is best for the implementer or other responsible person to contact the monitors directly for feedback and have them contact the person responsible with their observations when they feel it is necessary.

Another good idea is to distill their observations and report them with quotes in the telecommuting newsletter or whatever publicity methods are being used. This will help keep your monitors interested and the communications flowing. If the monitors report problems, it is a good idea to include them with solutions in the newsletter. If solutions are not readily apparent, it is best not to print the problems.

## Monitoring for Evaluation Data Gathering

Monitoring as a data-gathering method for an evaluation process is a structured technique that incorporates elements of the previous goals and can augment their achievement as well. Some approaches use a checklist that can be distributed and returned or completed in a phone interview.

Companies must decide which employees to survey. The telecommuters and their supervisors are usually high on the list, probably the next layer of management as well. It is also advisable to include colleagues who are not telecommuting. Some companies even survey customers.

The data-gathering checklist should be a combination of both support and evaluation questions. Questions for the telecommuter should be a mix of the following:

- What types of problems are you experiencing?
- Are you finding that the equipment in your home office is adequate for the tasks you have been assigned?
- Have you become more productive?
- Do you feel an increase in job satisfaction?

Supervisors' questions might include:

- How well is the telecommuter meeting his or her objectives and mileposts?
- Have you had any problems with communications between the telecommuter and his or her nontelecommuting colleagues?

The monitoring questions are much more specific than the ones to support telecommuters. The main difference between monitoring questions and actual evaluation questions is often only the use of more quantifiable answers, either in terms of numbers or some type of Likert-scale mechanism, so that some type of statistical analysis can be done.

At the end of the chapter we've included a couple of survey forms that were used for both monitoring and evaluation to give you an example of some of the questions that might be asked. (See appendix B.) After reading them you may be a bit confused about how this form of monitoring and an evaluation differ. Basically, the data you gather for both are the same. The two major differences are evaluation is a periodic process that usually results in a formal report of findings and recommendations with quantifiable questions as the norm, whereas monitoring occurs continuously and does not result in a formal report.

Almost anyone can undertake monitoring as long as the questions are fairly specific. Managers, secretaries, people hired directly for this purpose, and even the telecommuters themselves can be good monitors. However, I've found it just as effective, and probably more efficient, to simply create a good survey and send it through the mail or e-mail. Follow-up phone calls may be necessary to get some people to respond, but the mail survey technique works just as well as personal calls and visits if monitoring is only for evaluation data.

After determining the goals, what to ask, whom to ask, and who will do the asking, the two keys to successful monitoring are timing and getting it done. Timing is simply a matter of deciding when and how often to monitor. I recommend that monitoring for support and communications begins early, probably within the first month of the implementation, and that it be continuous. Evaluation monitoring should begin a bit later, after telecommuters have had some experience, but not too much later or it will become evaluation and not monitoring.

Getting it done may be the hardest aspect of monitoring. There always seems to be something to do that's more urgent. My advice is to use tried-and-true time management principles by scheduling for the process and making sure that it becomes the top priority at the scheduled time. It's often necessary to remind monitors that it is time and remind them of their responsibility. It doesn't do the program, the telecommuters, or the company any good to forgo monitoring.

# Evaluation of the Telecommuting Initiative

A formal evaluation is necessary to complete the intervention, particularly if a company is to call telecommuting a success. An evaluation is the only way a company can learn if it met its organizational need or achieved the expected group of advantages.

Companies undertake evaluations with a specific purpose in mind. Usually the reason is to determine if the intervention has met its goals, although some evaluations add other aspects to the why statement. Most companies use the goals they developed for the telecommuting vision, explained in chapter 3.

The number of goals and objectives a company may evaluate varies with its telecommuting initiative. Typically the goals and objectives fall into four or five general categories:
- telecommuter productivity and performance
- telecommuter and supervisor satisfaction with the program
- achievement of corporate internal goals
- achievement of corporate external goals
- cost-benefit analysis.

In some cases, a company may have no other internal goals than a cost-benefit analysis or employee satisfaction. If that's the case, internal goals would not constitute a category. Before the company discards internal goals as a category, however, it is advisable to explore other possible internal goals in the vision statement.

## Telecommuter Productivity and Performance

An evaluation of telecommuter productivity and performance often may be rather subjective. Although some companies have objective measures of productivity and performance, they are often too general to be useful or not specific enough to reflect what telecommuters are actually doing. Companies that have applicable productivity data can certainly use them, but anecdotal data are often all that is possible. Telecommuters and supervisors often give anecdotal data when they are asked for their opinions.

It is also possible by doing a comparison between the productivity of telecommuters and their colleagues who remain in the office. This approach is a bit suspect unless both groups are doing pretty much the same tasks in the same time frames. A comparison can produce some good information if the procedure is not too formal and gathers anecdotal data.

One simple but useful method is to ask the telecommuters and their supervisors to estimate a productivity percentage increase or decrease. I've also asked supervisors for a productivity percentage difference between telecommuters and nontelecommuters, although many of them are not comfortable with that question. Other questions you might ask related to telecommuter productivity appear in appendix A at the end of this chapter.

## Telecommuter and Supervisor Satisfaction With the Program

This category covers evaluations of feelings and is almost totally subjective in nature. The technique I employ most often is a simple yes-no question like, "Are you satisfied with the telecommuting process?" For evaluations that require a deeper level of information I add a why or why not to the question. It is possible to add some comparison data to the process by asking telecommuters if their job satisfaction level is higher now than before they were telecommuters. Similarly, it is possible to ask supervisors if they have seen an increase in the job satisfaction of their telecommuters or if they think the telecommuters are satisfied with telecommuting. Some companies also ask supervisors if they were more satisfied with their job because of telecommuting, although I'm not sure what the point of this is because the main purpose of telecommuting interventions is seldom to increase supervisors' job satisfaction.

Another approach is to ask telecommuters to state whether they have met the personal goals for telecommuting that they developed earlier in the program.

Evaluations often do not look at the effect of telecommuting on the telecommuter's family life. This is an important consideration, but can be a very sensitive issue, particularly if the wrong person is doing the evaluating. Because the data delve deeply into personal matters, the company should not know or have access to them, and they do not belong in personnel files or supervision records. It is advisable to hire an outside evaluator to assist with this part of the telecommuting evaluation because disinterested third parties have no unfavorable personnel or supervisory relationship. They do not normally communicate with other people in the organization, so employees won't see them as a threat to tell tales. Outside evaluators can keep this entire aspect private by not naming names, but by simply reporting general trends. The data that come from an outside evaluation are likely to be more valid than if the evaluation were done by an insider because they are not filtered by an insider's knowledge of the processes and organization.

Surveys are probably as effective as any other approach to obtain information for this category of evaluation. Appendix B provides samples of some satisfaction questions from evaluations that companies performed for both the telecommuter and the supervisor. Telephone calls and personal visits work well too, but they are more time consuming.

## Achievement of Corporate Internal Goals

Increased employee job satisfaction and decreasing cost may actually fall under this category, particularly if it was a goal of the program. It is possible to evaluate it here or in its own category. Other internal goals might include the following:
- reduced turnover
- decreased absenteeism
- reduced sick time expenses
- reduced employee stress
- decreased lateness
- increased ability to attract nonlocal candidates for job openings
- number of telecommuters
- number of hours employees telecommute.

Companies' personnel and payroll departments keep many of the statistics that pertain to internal goals, so it's easier to gather objective data on them than on many other goals. Some areas won't show an improvement in the first or even second evaluation cycle. In the first place, many of these aspects take time, and in the second, there are a lot of other mitigating factors, such as changes in hiring practices, restructuring, human resources policies or procedures, and environmental changes. Besides, these are goals to strive for. If they are all reached in the first evaluation, then the program aimed too low.

One word of caution: The evaluation should measure corporate goals set forth in the telecommuting vision statement, not simply things it can gather data about. The worst approach I ever saw was an intervention in which the consultant evaluators assigned hoped-for percentage changes to some of these items when they were not part of the goals. Either way they lost. If the intervention didn't reach the percentages, the program was a failure. If it did, the "after the fact" nature of the percentage gains made it look like the whole evaluation was a setup, one of those drawing the target around the arrow processes.

It is possible to obtain anecdotal data on this category by asking the supervisors and telecommuters for their perceptions. Some sample questions appear in appendix A.

## Achievement of Corporate External Goals

This category is probably the easiest to evaluate. External goals are those that affect the community. Good objective data are relatively simple to develop and directly reflect how the corporation is doing its part in reducing miles traveled, gasoline used, pollutants discharged, and the like. Statistics for the ADA and EEO may go here or in the internal category. Companies typically use calculations like the following to produce data for this category. These statistics are based on the current national averages of 15 commuting miles one way and two days' telecommuting time per week.

- average decrease in mile commuted per telecommuter: 3,000 a year
- average personal time gain for a telecommuter: 100 hours a year
- average gas savings for an employee telecommuting two days a week: 250 gallons per year
- average reduction in carbon monoxide per day of telecommuting: 192 pounds
- average reduction of unburned hydrocarbons per day: 36 pounds
- average reduction of particulate matter introduced into the air per day: 0.8 pounds.

## Cost-Benefit Analysis

This category is normally the primary emphasis of a telecommuting evaluation process. Companies typically design their telecommuting interventions to realize some cost savings over those of their previous workplace system. At worst, companies do not expect to lose money as they increase intangibles such as employee satisfaction. Actual cost savings may be due to increased productivity, decreased staffing needs (such as in a call center), or the most usual reason, decreased physical plant requirements, such as office space.

A cost-benefit analysis should be objective. There should be data generated for expenses and data for cost savings. If this is the first planned evaluation of a telecommuting initiative, the expenses might be amortized to show how much of the cost of telecommuting has been recouped so far and actual cost savings expected to occur.

The company should have determined the basis of its cost-benefit analysis when it was exploring the concept of telecommuting and developing its procedures. A number of books, articles, and other assorted information are available on the methodology of cost-benefit analyses. The evaluation technique consists mostly of gathering the data required by the cost-benefit analysis plan, analyzing them, and writing a report.

Following are typical components of a cost-benefit analysis with representative figures:

- training: averages about $300 per telecommuter
- furniture: intervention specific
- equipment: average $3,500 if all purchased new
- moving expenses: company specific
- telephone bills: approximately $60 above in-office costs
- administrative: $700 per telecommuter for start-up, and approximately $80 per telecommuter per year for ongoing.

One company I worked with used $4,500 as its estimated expenditure for setting up a telecommuter and $2,500 as the yearly tab for maintaining each telecommuter. These estimates are useful for a simplified cost-benefit analysis.

Some companies may wish to add the following figures to their estimates:

- average productivity increase: $350 per month per telecommuter
- decreased sick leave usage: three days per telecommuter per year
- decreased medical costs: hard to determine but can be significant
- decreased turnover: average 20 percent among telecommuters
- reduced need for office space: average reduction in a fully implemented program may be 33 percent of a company's cost per square foot
- decreased energy consumption in buildings: no averages available

There are also decreased costs for the telecommuters including gas, parking, car maintenance, food, and dry cleaning, which could be figured into a cost-benefit analysis. These should be figured against a roughly $300 to $500 a year loss a telecommuter will incur for utilities and other expenses.

Studies indicate that companies will have a negative cost-benefit ratio for the first year and possibly even the second, but double digit positive ratios are not uncommon by the fifth year of a successful intervention. (Descriptions of studies cited in this chapter appear in some of the books listed in the suggested readings at the end of this book.)

## Independent Evaluators

There are other things to consider in an evaluation process. One of these is the need for an independent evaluator. Although people in the organization who are closest to the telecommuting process would be good evaluators for a number of reasons—they know the system, have the ability to act on problems, have rapport with telecommuters and supervisors—there are a number of reasons why they would not be good evaluators—they have a vested interest, are too close to the process, are unable to deal objectively with possible personal failures.

There is no right or wrong answer to the question of who should be responsible for the telecommuting evaluation. An observer with an academic bent would probably recommend that companies use impartial observers and evaluators. The cost associated with this approach and business considerations such as strangers looking into personnel and payroll data would suggest the opposite. We noted earlier that for some items such as the effect of telecommuting on the telecommuters' families an independent evaluator is almost required. This might also be true for some of the company's internal business goals, particularly those that relate to personnel or supervisory aspects that can be points of contention for some individuals and even entire departments.

My recommendation is to combine the methods where possible. If it is possible to implement aspects of the evaluation plan with internal staff and not compromise the data, do it. It is less expensive and has some of the advantages we just mentioned. Use external resources when an internal evaluator would be suspect or if there is a question about the objectivity of internal evaluation. The evaluation is too important and too closely related to the overall success of the intervention to take any chances.

## Customer Evaluations of Telecommuting

Companies may wish to use customers as part of the telecommuting evaluation. This approach is advisable for companies that are heavily involved in customer service (and which aren't?). Because companies' internal operations should be invisible to its customers, companies wouldn't want to ask what customers think of the telecommuters or the telecommuting program. The best ways to phrase these questions are to ask if response time is better, if service is better, or if they've seen any changes in the organization in the past four months, or whatever the applicable number. It is important to phrase the questions to allow for both positive and negative responses.

Even telecommuters who do not have external customer service responsibilities in all likelihood have internal customers. A sample customer evaluation form appears in appendix B.

## Evaluation Data From Telecommuting Training

Evaluation data are also available from before and after interviews of supervisors and telecommuters during their training process. If this is done normally to check on the effectiveness of the training, you can use some aspects of the data these interviews (or questionnaires) provide in your general evaluation. If you don't do this as part of your normal training practice…you should.

## The Evaluation Report

In the end, what the evaluation is trying to determine, no matter what is being evaluated, or who does it, or how, is if the targets for the intervention were met. These targets can be as concrete as dollars of cost savings or as ethereal as employee satisfaction. The evaluation report states first and foremost which targets were met and which were not, and it analyzes why.

The report should also explore any ways in which the outcomes differed from what was expected—even if the differences benefited the company—and why. The reasons may be unrealistic goals, expectations that were too high or poorly defined, or inadequate support throughout the organization. These aspects of the program need to be revisited and possibly revised. That would require returning to the beginning of the intervention, but that is what evaluation is for, to close the loop.

In telecommuting, as in everything else, it is possible to learn from failures, and particularly in telecommuting, individual failure. I have often seen telecommuting evaluation reports that had plenty of analysis based on overall data, but nothing on the individual telecommuters themselves. If a company loses even one telecommuter, it needs to ask, why? Was it less than adequate training, start-up difficulties, problems with the technology, selection deficiencies, supervisory difficulties, or possibly something that couldn't be controlled?

If it turns out that a telecommuter isn't cut out for that kind of work, it is best to move the employee back to the office, as quickly and quietly as possible. The organization will have incurred a resource loss in terms of the time and money spent training and setting up the failed telecommuter, but for the individual it should be as seamless as simply changing offices.

## Conclusion

The completion of the evaluation report brings the company full circle in its telecommuting intervention. Lessons learned in evaluation will help the company revise the initiative's procedures and possibly even the goals, create changes in the training and in the successfulness of the current telecommuters and those who become telecommuters later. As more become telecommuters, there will be more monitoring and evaluation.

If I could leave you with one thought it would be one of the major themes of this book: Successful telecommuting is dependent upon a comprehensive analysis that determines the vision, objectives, and procedures that will make the intervention effective. Or, to paraphrase an old saying, all's well that begins well.

# Appendix A

# Questions for Monitoring Productivity, Satisfaction, Supervisors, and Internal Goals

## Questions Related to Productivity

Note that questions preceded by an asterisk (*) can be asked of supervisors as well, with some rewording.

*Has the quantity of your work increased?

*Do you believe the quality of your work has increased?

Has the amount of time you spend actually working increased or decreased?

Do you have fewer distractions when you are working at home?

How often do you find yourself less productive because you do not have the support tools you need at home?

Does the lack of face-to-face interaction with your co-workers decrease your productivity?

*From a productivity and performance point of view, do you feel you are a successful telecommuter?

*Are you maintaining adequate communications with your supervisor?

*Do you feel your performance problems have decreased due to telecommuting?

*Do you feel you are less accessible as a telecommuter?

Has the amount of supervision you receive increased or decreased due to telecommuting?

*Have you found your productivity decreasing due to mechanical problems with your home hardware?

*Are problems with timely delivery of mail reducing your productivity?

*Do you feel you've been successful at staying visible?

*Do you think your creativity has increased due to telecommuting?

*Do you feel you are a more effective employee since you began to telecommute?

## Questions Related to Satisfaction

Have you achieved your primary personal goal for telecommuting?

What other personal goals have you achieved through telecommuting? (Note that the three most common responses are cut commuting time, work at own pace, and save transportation costs.)

Has your feeling of satisfaction with your work increased or decreased since you began telecommuting?

Have you been more satisfied with your home life since you began telecommuting?

Are you feeling less job-related stress?

Do you believe you are working too long on your telecommuting days?

Do you feel isolated from your co-workers due to telecommuting?

Do you feel you are a successful telecommuter?

Are you satisfied with telecommuting?

Do you feel your supervisor views telecommuting favorably?

Do you feel your chances for advancement have been reduced due to being a telecommuter?

Are you spending more time with your family?

Have you experienced any telecommuting-based psychological problems since you became a telecommuter?

Do you feel your colleagues respect what you are doing as a telecommuter?

Do you feel your in-office colleagues may be jealous of the flexibility you have as a telecommuter?

Are you having any problems with workaholism?

## Supervisor Questions

Are you satisfied with telecommuting?

Are you comfortable in assessing the work performance of your telecommuters?

Are you able to maintain adequate communications with your telecommuters?

Are you able to maintain a sense of teamwork in the department?

Do you find it more difficult to manage telecommuters than in-office employees?

Do you find it more difficult to handle performance problems with telecommuters?

Do you feel you have less control with you telecommuters?

Do you find that the extra coordination needed for telecommuters is not worth the results you are getting?

Are you finding any jealousy issues between your telecommuters and their in-office colleagues?

## Questions Related to the Achievement of Corporate Internal Goals

Do you feel telecommuting has decreased absenteeism?

Do you feel telecommuting has reduced lateness in your group?

Do you think telecommuting has had any effect on your ability to retain employees?

Do you feel telecommuting has had any effect on your ability to hire qualified individuals?

# Appendix B

# Sample Evaluation Surveys

## Customer Evaluation Form

Name _____

Date _____

Thank you for taking a few minutes to complete this survey. This survey will help us measure the success of our telecommuting program.

1.  Have you noticed any changes in your interactions with your customer service representative?

    ☐ Yes

    ☐ No

2.  Currently, how easy is it to interact with your customer service representative?

    ☐ Very easy

    ☐ Easy

    ☐ Difficult

    ☐ Very difficult

3.  How would you rate communications with your customer service representative?

    ☐ Very good

    ☐ Good

    ☐ Poor

    ☐ Very poor

4. How would you rate your written communication with your customer service representative?

   ☐ Very good

   ☐ Good

   ☐ Poor

   ☐ Very poor

5. How would you rate telephone communication with your customer service representative?

   ☐ Very good

   ☐ Good

   ☐ Poor

   ☐ Very poor

6. Currently, how responsive is your customer service representative to your requests?

   ☐ Very fast

   ☐ Fast

   ☐ Slow

   ☐ Very slow

7. Overall, our customer service has

   ☐ Improved

   ☐ Stayed the same

   ☐ Declined

8. Please add any comments you wish to make here.


THANK YOU!

# Manager's Evaluation of Telecommuting

Name _____

Date _____

Much of the success of our telecommuting program depends on you. We need your feedback to help us determine how the program is running. Please take a few minutes to fill out this survey.

1. Have you noticed any performance changes in your telecommuting employees?

    ☐ Their performance has improved.

    ☐ Their performance has remained pretty much the same.

    ☐ Their performance has deteriorated.

2. Have you noticed a change in their work ethic or attitude toward work?

    ☐ It has generally improved.

    ☐ It has generally remained the same.

    ☐ It has generally fallen.

3. How have communications with your telecommuting employee(s) changed?

    ☐ Improved

    ☐ Stayed the same

    ☐ Worsened

4. How are your employees performing in relation to their objectives?

    ☐ Better

    ☐ The same

    ☐ Worse

5. In general, how is telecommuting working for you and your group?

   ☐ Very well

   ☐ Not too well

   ☐ Badly

6. What could be done to improve the telecommuting program?

7. Please comment on your answers to these questions or any other aspects of the telecommuting program here.

## Telecommuter's Evaluation of Telecommuting

Name _____

Date _____

Please help us to have the best possible telecommuting program by taking a few minutes to fill out this survey. Your assistance is appreciated!

1. Has telecommuting made your job easier?

   ☐ Yes

   ☐ No

2. Has your productivity been enhanced?

   ☐ A lot

   ☐ Some

   ☐ None

3. Consider the number of hours you work now versus when you were not telecommuting. To achieve your objectives, are you working:

   ☐ More hours

   ☐ About the same number

   ☐ Fewer hours

4. How would you rate communication with your manager?

   ☐ Better

   ☐ About the same

   ☐ Not as good

5. How would you rate communication with your colleagues?

   ☐ Better

   ☐ About the same

   ☐ Not as good

6. How would you rate communication with your customers (internal as well as external)?

   ☐ Better

   ☐ About the same

   ☐ Not as good

7. Now that you are not in the office as much, do you find it difficult to get support from other employees in doing your job?

   ☐ Yes

   ☐ No

8. How would you rate your job satisfaction relative to before you telecommuted?

   ☐ Much more satisfied

   ☐ Somewhat more satisfied

   ☐ Less satisfied

   ☐ Much less satisfied

9. Do you feel telecommuting has improved the quality of your work?

   ☐ Yes

   ☐ No

10. Has telecommuting improved your quality of life?

☐ Yes

☐ No

☐ It has lessened it.

11. Now that you've tried it, would telecommuting be something you would look for if you were considering working at another company?

☐ Yes

☐ No

☐ Would make little difference

12. In general, how well is telecommuting working for you?

☐ It's working well.

☐ It's not working.

☐ I've not been able to make a decision about it yet.

13. On a scale of 1 to 10, my current job satisfaction level is

1  2  3  4  5  6  7  8  9  10

14. What could be done to improve the telecommuting program?

# Glossary

**Americans With Disabilities Act (ADA):** Federal regulation that requires that people with disabilities have equal access to jobs and an accessible physical working environment. Telecommuting satisfies the law in many situations by allowing employees with disabilities to work at home.

**Compensatory time:** Hours worked but not paid that will be used as time off later. As with compressed workweek, this arrangement is usually not a telecommuting process, but it may be depending on the telecommuters' compensation procedures. Companies must decide on this policy before beginning telecommuting.

**Compressed workweek:** A variation on a typical work schedule in which employees work the standard number of hours in fewer than the standard number of days. Typically, employees work four 10-hour days, rather than five eight-hour days. Telecommuting may incorporate some aspects of a compressed workweek, depending on how telecommuters' pay is calculated and the freedom workers have to choose their own work time.

**Computer-based training (CBT):** A general term used to describe any learning event that uses computers as the primary distribution method; typically used to refer primarily to text-based computer-delivered training.

**Computer conferencing:** Conferencing or communications among groups of individuals using computers as the medium and normally done asynchronously.

**Core time:** A process in which employees are expected to be at the main work location for a predetermined number of hours, but spend the rest of the normal workweek elsewhere. This is a precursor to telecommuting in which the rest of the time is spent at home, and the core time may be as little as a day or two a month.

**Electronic bulletin board services (EBBS):** Asynchronous system for electronically leaving messages for others using computer networks.

**Electronic mail (e-mail):** The exchange of messages through computers.

**Equal Employment Opportunity (EEO):** A collective term for U.S. laws directed at producing equality in the workplace.

**Ergonomics:** The study of designing machines or processes based on the human body so workers are more comfortable and efficient while working.

**Facsimile (fax) machine:** Technological device that translates words and graphics on a page of paper into a data stream and transmits that data stream via regular phone lines to a receiver, usually another fax machine, though possibly a computer. The receiver translates the data stream back to graphics and words.

**Flextime:** Flextime usually requires an employee to spend a normal number of hours in the office each day, but allows some choice in what those hours are. This might include arriving early, leaving late, or being away sometime in the middle of the normal workday. Flextime is not a telecommuting process as the telecommuter by definition spends entire days away from the office. Flextime may be an aspect of telecommuting if the telecommuters have the choice of what days they will telecommute or what hours they will be available in their home offices.

**Graphical user interface (GUI):** A system for interfacing with a computer in which the user is keyed into functions and processes through images, often known as icons, rather than through printed word messages that appear on the computer screen.

**Groupware:** An integrated computer application that supports collaborative group efforts through the sharing of calendars for project management and scheduling, collective document preparation, e-mail handling, shared database access, electronic meetings, and other activities.

**Hardware:** Physical equipment a telecommuter uses.

**Hoteling:** Office space on a temporary basis for employees whose job requires geographic proximity to a certain area, possibly including space in the company's current facility or short-term leased space in a facility unrelated to the company. The company may reserve the space for periods of time or utilize it on a drop-in basis. Although hoteling is not considered a telecommuting process, companies use the same technology for telecommuters' home offices as they do for hotel offices at noncorporate locations.

**Internet:** A loose confederation of computer networks around the world connected through several primary networks.

**Intranet:** A general term describing any network contained within an organization, primarily networks that use Internet technology.

**ISDN (integrated services digital network) line:** A high-speed data communications line connecting two or more computers via modems. ISDN lines can carry more information than regular phone lines and are thus considered faster for data transfer.

**Job sharing:** A system in which two or more employees share one normal workweek job and the commensurate pay.

**Local area network (LAN):** A network of computers sharing the resources of a single processor or server within a relatively small geographic area.

**Management information system (MIS) department:** The usual department or group within an organization charged with the development and maintenance of the company's computer and technological assets.

**Modem:** A computer add-on that permits computer-to-computer transfer of data over common telephone and special data lines.

**Notebook (laptop) computers:** Common terms for any of a series of portable computers. These computers can be easily moved from place to place and may even have wireless connection capabilities with other computers and computer networks.

**Remote work (telework) centers:** Corporate-owned minifacilities away from the main office, usually in the suburbs when the main office is an intercity location. Unlike telecommuters, employees at these facilities are not working from home and are expected to be at these centers or the main office each day.

**Satellite officing:** Offices that a corporation owns or leases for a long term but that are not at the main headquarters. Satellite offices can be as small as single rooms or as large as a building floor. Most often they are for permanent use by specified employees, although companies may use them for hoteling as well. Satellite offices are often synonymous with remote work centers, but some organizations define each differently. Like employees at remote work centers, employees are expected to normally be at the satellite office and not at home. A satellite office may be the place that a telecommuter reports to on nontelecommuting days.

**Shared space:** The use of a single office by more than one employee, though not physically simultaneously (or so it is hoped). Telecommuters who usually report to the main facility on a scheduled, periodic basis can easily share an office. This is one of the real estate advantages of telecommuting, but one of the psychological disadvantages. Scheduling is a major concern with this process.

**Software:** The programs that make a computer capable of performing various functions such as communications, word processing, and data processing.

**Task analysis:** The process of analyzing a job and the tasks associated with that job to discover the skills and knowledge necessary to do the tasks. Task analysis is the foundation process for all good training programs.

**Team spacing (group address):** A process that has become more prevalent with the ascendancy of teams, team spacing provides team members with a group space that is a combination office and team meeting area instead of offices. Unlike shared space, team spacing presents no scheduling problems because there are often no desks or other accoutrements of a normal office. Because telecommuting can include a virtual team process, team spacing can be an aspect of it.

**Telecommuting:** The combination of various aspects of shared space, flextime, and electronic communications to increase worker productivity.

**Telecommuting contract:** A document that telecommuters and their supervisors usually develop that outlines the roles and responsibilities of both during the telecommuting process. It may also include information concerning the responsibilities of the company as a whole.

**Teleconferencing:** The instantaneous exchange of audio, video, or text between two or more individuals or groups at two or more locations.

**Videoconferencing:** Usually the same concept as teleconferencing, although teleconferencing is sometimes reserved for situations that are not connected with a computer, whereas videoconferencing usually means a computer connection as well as the camera.

**Virtual office:** An alternative work process in which an employee has no actual physical location for an office, but "plugs in" from wherever he or she happens to be. This may include a hotel room, home, a conference room, or even a car. Salespeople often have a virtual office. Because this book focuses on home offices at which employees perform office work on a regular basis, it does not consider virtual offices to be telecommuting functions or salespeople to be telecommuters.

**Voice mail:** An automated electronic telephone answering system.

**Wide area network (WAN):** A network of computers sharing the resources of a single processor or server over a relatively large geographic area.

**Wireless technology:** General term for machines and processes that allow transmission of voice, pictures, and data without the use of a physical medium such as wire or cable. Usually the process works by microwave transmission.

# Suggested Readings and Other Resources

## Books

Alvarez, Mark. *The Home Office Book: How to Set Up and Use an Efficient Personal Workspace in the Computer Age.* Woodbury, CT: Goodwind Press, 1990.

Bredin, Alice. *The Virtual Office Survival Handbook: What Telecommuters and Entrepreneurs Need to Succeed in Today's Non Traditional Workplace.* New York: John Wiley, 1996.

Fleming, Lisa. *The One-Minute Commuter: How to Keep Your Job and Stay at Home Telecommuting.* New York: Fleming Ltd., 1990.

Gordon, Gil E., & Marcia Kelly. *Telecommuting: How to Make It Work for You and Your Company.* Englewood Cliffs, NJ: Prentice Hall, 1986.

Gray, M., N. Hodson, & Gil Gordon. *Teleworking Explained.* New York: John Wiley, 1993.

Kanorek, Lisa. *Organizing Your Home Office for Success.* San Francisco: New American Library/Plume, 1993.

Kugelmass, Joel. *Telecommuting: A Manager's Guide to Flexible Work Arrangements.* Lexington, KY: Lexington Books, 1995.

Langendoen, David, & Dan Costa, editors. *The Home Office Computing Handbook.* New York: Windcrest/McGraw-Hill, 1994.

Langhoff, June. *Telecom Made Easy* (2d edition). Newport, RI: Aegis Publishing Group, 1996.

Laqueur, Maria, & Donna Dickinson. *Breaking Out of 9 to 5: How to Redesign Your Job to Fit You.* Princeton, NJ: Peterson's Guides, 1994.

Leonhard, Woody. *The Underground Guide to Telecommuting: Slightly Askew Advice on Leaving the Rat Race Behind.* New York: Addison-Wesley, 1995.

Mahfood, Phillip E. *Home Work: How to Hire, Manage and Monitor Employees Who Work at Home.* Seattle: Probus, 1992.

Meade, Jeff. *Home Sweet Office.* Princeton, NJ: Peterson's Guides, 1993.

Nilles, Jack M. *Making Telecommuting Happen: A Guide for Telemanagers and Telecommuters.* New York: Van Nostrand Reinhold, 1994.

Olmsted, Barney, & Suzanne Smith. *Creating a Flexible Workplace: How to Select and Manage Alternative Work Options.* New York: AMACOM, 1988.

Schepp, Brad, & Debra Schepp. *The Telecommuter's Handbook: How to Work for a Salary Without Ever Leaving the House* (2d edition). New York: McGraw-Hill, 1995.

## Magazines

*Home Office,* 2392 Morse Avenue, Irvine, CA 92614.

*Home Office Computing,* 411 Lafayette Street, New York, NY 10003; 1.800.288.7812.

*Mobile Office,* 470 Park Avenue South, New York, NY 10016; 1.800.274.1218.

## Newsletters

*The Digital Workplace,* Institute for the Study of Distributed Work, 725 Washington Street, Suite 210, Oakland, CA 94607; phone: 1.510.834.1485; e-mail: ISDW@aol.com.

*Telecommuting Review,* Gil Gordon Associates, 10 Donner Court, Monmouth Junction, NJ 08852; phone: 908.329.2266.

## Associations

TAC: The International Teleworkers Association, 204 E Street, N.E., Washington, DC 20002; phone: 202.547.6157; e-mail: www.telecommute.org.

# About the Author

George M. Piskurich has been in the training profession in various industry settings for over 20 years. A consultant in instructional design and technology-based training implementation, he is a principal at GMP Associates. His areas of special interest include self-directed learning, performance technology, customer service, and management and supervisory development. He has written extensively in his areas of interest, presented at various national and international conferences on topics ranging from mentoring systems to interactive distance learning, and has served in a number of capacities for the American Society for Training & Development (ASTD) and the International Society for Performance Improvement (ISPI). Piskurich received a Ph.D. in instructional design from the University of Pittsburgh. He lives in the Raleigh/Durham area of North Carolina and can be reached at 919.968.0878; e-mail: GMP1@Compuserve.com.